The Cold War and Beyond

Chronology of the United States Air Force, 1947–1997

Frederick J. Shaw Jr.
Timothy Warnock

Air Force History and Museums Program
in association with
Air University Press

1997

For sale by the U.S. Government Printing Office
Superintendent of Documents, Mail Stop: SSOP, Washington, DC 20402-9328
ISBN 0-16-049145-2

Contents

Foreword

This chronology commemorates the golden anniversary of the establishment of the United States Air Force (USAF) as an independent service. Dedicated to the men and women of the USAF past, present, and future, it records significant events and achievements from 18 September 1947 through 9 April 1997.

Since its establishment, the USAF has played a significant role in the events that have shaped modern history. Initially, the reassuring drone of USAF transports announced the aerial lifeline that broke the Berlin blockade, the Cold War's first test of wills. In the tense decades that followed, the USAF deployed a strategic force of nuclear-capable intercontinental bombers and missiles that deterred open armed conflict between the United States and the Soviet Union. During the Cold War's deadly flash points, USAF jets roared through the skies of Korea and Southeast Asia, wresting air superiority from their communist opponents and bringing air power to the support of friendly ground forces. In the great global competition for the hearts and minds of the Third World, hundreds of USAF humanitarian missions relieved victims of war, famine, and natural disaster. The Air Force performed similar disaster relief services on the home front. Over Grenada, Panama, and Libya, the USAF participated in key contingency actions that presaged post–Cold War operations.

In the aftermath of the Cold War the USAF became deeply involved in constructing a new world order. As the Soviet Union disintegrated, USAF flights succored the populations of the newly independent states. Blazing across the Iraqi skies, Desert Storm's aerial assault paved the way for the liberation of Kuwait and established the leadership of the United States in an emerging global coalition. Since then, the USAF has shielded Iraqi Kurds, relieved populations on the verge of starvation, supported the restoration of democracy in Haiti, and reestablished the authority of United Nations peacekeepers in the former Republic of Yugoslavia.

Tremendous technological changes have accompanied the USAF's first 50 years. Supersonic jets swiftly succeeded the propeller-driven relics of World War II, only to be replaced by faster and more complex progeny. In-flight refueling extended the range and capabilities of tactical and strategic aircraft. Advanced imaging systems installed in high-altitude jets, unpiloted drones, and orbiting satellites have enhanced the effectiveness of aerial reconnaissance. The advent of the intercontinental ballistic missile introduced a new and more terrible dimension to strategic deterrence. Over the same period the USAF advanced into space, as its people launched the first satellites, explored the moon, and crewed space shuttles.

The USAF's first 50 years also spanned a period of profound change in the society of the United States—change that has influenced the service's composition and policies. Opportunities for professional advancement have opened to all. Participating in the full range of military specialties, minorities and women now occupy some of the highest command positions. The diverse composition of the modern USAF, coupled with open opportunity, has paid off in greater internal cohesion and effectiveness and the fresh perspectives required to successfully pursue global engagement far into the twenty-first century.

Taken individually, each entry in this volume marks a single, notable moment in the evolution of an illustrious heritage. In the aggregate, the entries tell a remarkable story of a powerful military institution's adaptation to 50 years of political, technological, and social change.

DR. FREDERICK J. SHAW JR.
Chief, Research Division
Air Force Historical Research Agency

CHRONOLOGY

1947-1956

1947

18 September: W. Stuart Symington is sworn in as the first Secretary of the Air Force. Effective date of transfer of air activities from Army to new Department of the Air Force.

25 September: President Harry S. Truman names Gen Carl A. Spaatz as the first U.S. Air Force (USAF) chief of staff.

26 September: Defense Secretary James W. Forrestal orders the transfer of personnel, bases, and materiel from the Army to the new Department of the Air Force.

14 October: The first faster-than-sound flight is made by Capt Charles E. Yeager at Muroc Air Base (AB), California, in a rocket-powered USAF research plane, Bell XS–1 rocket ship. Captain Yeager wins the Mackay Trophy for the most meritorious flight of the year.

The rocket-powered Bell X–1 became the first aircraft to break the sound barrier, with Capt Charles E. "Chuck" Yeager at the controls. The X–1 shown here is in its first powered flight, with Chalmers "Slick" Goodlin as pilot, shortly after having been dropped from its B–29 mother ship.

24 November: The first live Aerobee rocket fires to a height of 190,000 feet from White Sands Proving Ground, New Mexico. The Aerobee is a liquid-fueled missile used to research atmospheric conditions up to 70 miles above the earth.

17 December: A prototype B–47 Stratojet medium bomber flies for the first time at Seattle, Washington. Operational variants of this prototype have a combat radius in excess of 1,500 nautical miles and an average cruise speed in excess of 400 miles per hour (mph).

1948

30 January: Orville Wright dies in Dayton, Ohio, at age 76.

20 February: The Strategic Air Command receives its first B–50 Superfortress bomber. Equipped for in-flight refueling, the B–50 is an improved version of the B–29 with larger engines and a taller tail fin and rudder.

26 April: The U.S. Air Force becomes the first service to plan for racial integration, anticipating President Truman's executive order to be issued in July 1948.

1 June: U.S. Navy and Air Force air transport systems consolidate into Military Air Transport Service (MATS) under the United States Air Force.

12 June: Congress passes the Women's Armed Service Integration Act, establishing Women in the Air Force (WAF).

16 June: The U.S. Air Force appoints Col Geraldine P. May as the first WAF director.

26 June: The Berlin airlift (Operation Vittles) begins as a response to a ground blockade imposed by the Soviet Union on Berlin.

26 June: SAC's 7th Bombardment Group receives the first operational B–36 Peacemaker heavy bomber. With a length of 160 feet and wings spanning 230 feet, the Peacemaker is the world's largest bomber with intercontinental capability.

20 July: Sixteen F–80 Shooting Stars reach Scotland from Selfridge Field, Michigan, after nine hours, 20 minutes,

U.S. Air Force C–47s await unloading at Templehof Air Base, Germany. The USAF maintained an airborne lifeline of food and fuel to West Berliln during the Berlin airlift in 1948–49.

accomplishing the first west-to-east transatlantic flight by jet planes.

23 July: The Military Airlift Transport Service is ordered to establish Airlift Task Force with headquarters in Germany for relief to Berlin. Maj Gen William H. Tunner is named to command Task Force operations.

30 July: The USAF takes delivery of its first jet bomber, the North American Aviation B–45A Tornado. This light bomber is a tactical aircraft and later will be the first USAF aircraft to carry a tactical nuclear bomb.

6 August: The first B–29 Superfortresses to circumnavigate the globe land near Tucson, Arizona, after a leisurely 15-day trip.

10 November: The School of Aviation Medicine, Randolph Air Force Base (AFB), Texas, holds the first symposium on space medicine.

30 November: Curtiss-Wright demonstrates its new reversible pitch propellers, enabling a C–54 to make a controlled descent from 15,000 to 1,000 feet—one minute, 22 seconds.

8 December: A six-engine B–36 completes a 9,400-mile nonstop flight, taking off from Fort Worth, Texas, flying to Hawaii, and returning to Texas without refueling.

9–28 December: On 9 December 1948 an arctic storm forces the crew of a C–47 Skytrain to land on the Greenland ice cap, stranding a crew of seven. Subsequent rescue attempts by a B–17 and a towed glider fail, stranding five rescuers as well. On 28 December Lt Col Emil Beaudry lands a ski-equipped Skytrain on the ice cap, rescuing the 12 airmen. For this rescue, Beaudry wins the Mackay Trophy.

17 December: On the 45th anniversary of the first heavier-than-air aircraft flight, the Smithsonian Institution celebrates the return of the Wright 1903 Flyer, also called the *Kitty Hawk*, to the United States. The plane arrived in Washington on 22 November from the British Museum, where it has been displayed for 20 years.

31 December: Allied aircraft log the 100,000th flight of the Berlin airlift.

1949

9 February: The Department of Space Medicine is established at the School of Aviation Medicine, Randolph AFB.

2 March: *Lucky Lady II* lands at Carswell AFB, Texas. Piloted by Capt James Gallagher, the B–50 Superfortress completes the first nonstop, around-the-world flight in history, covering 23,452 miles in 94 hours, one minute, refueling in the air over the Azores, Arabia, the Philippines, and Hawaii. The crew of the *Lucky Lady II* wins the Mackay Trophy for this flight.

26 March: A B–36 Peacemaker bomber equipped with ten engines—the usual six reciprocating, plus four jet—makes its first successful test flight at Fort Worth, Texas.

Secretary of the Air Force Stuart Symington congratulates the crew of the *Lucky Lady II* after their historic nonstop around-the-world flight in1949.

6 April: Curtiss-Wright announces the X–1 rocket plane (made by Bell, engine by Curtiss-Wright) flies at 1,000 mph, an unofficial world-record speed for piloted planes.

11 May: President Truman signs a bill providing a 3,000-mile guided-missile test range for USAF. The range is subsequently established at Cape Canaveral, Florida.

12 May: The Soviet Union ends the blockade of West Berlin. To build up stockpiles, airlift continues on a gradually reduced basis.

2 June: Gen Henry H. Arnold is given the permanent rank of General of the Air Force.

1 July: The Air Force establishes the USAF Medical Service, headed by Maj Gen Malcolm C. Grow, the first USAF surgeon general.

10 August: President Truman signs the National Security Act amendments of 1949, revising unification legislation of

1947 and converting the National Military Establishment into the Department of Defense (DOD).

30 September: The Berlin airlift, gradually reduced since 12 May 1949, officially ends. Allied aircraft carried 2,343,301.5 tons of supplies on 277,264 flights. U.S. planes carried 1,783,826 tons.

5 December: As result of detection of a Soviet atomic explosion in August 1949, USAF diverts $50 million from other projects to begin construction of radar sites in Alaska and other areas of the United States.

1950

15 January: General of the Air Force Henry H. Arnold dies of a heart ailment at Sonoma, California.

1 June: The USAF is authorized to organize the Ground Observer Corps as part of the civil air raid warning system.

The F–51 Mustang, a superb air superiority fighter by World War II standards, was relegated to ground attack a few years later in Korea, outclassed by new generations of jet fighters.

27 June: President Truman announces that he has ordered the USAF to aid South Korea, which North Korean communist forces had invaded two days previously.

27 June: 1st Lt William G. Hudson, USAF, flying an F–82 Twin Mustang, shoots down and destroys the first enemy plane in the Korean War, a Yak–11, a single-engine, propeller-driven Soviet fighter aircraft.

30 June: President Truman authorizes Gen Douglas MacArthur to dispatch air forces against targets in North Korea.

6 July: The Harmon International Aviation Awards Committee names James H. Doolittle as aviator of the decade, Jacqueline Cochran as outstanding aviatrix, and Vice Adm Charles E. Rosendahl as top aeronaut (lighter-than-air man).

13 July: B–29s of the 22d and 92d Bombardment Groups bomb the North Korean marshaling yards at Wonsan, the first strategic bombing raid of the Korean War. The groups had been alerted on 1 July, left the United States on 5 July, and arrived at their bases in Japan and Okinawa only six days prior to this raid.

5 August: Maj Louis J. Sebille, USAF, is killed in action flying a severely damaged F–51 Mustang against an enemy force concentration in Korea. Major Sebille is the first member of the recently created USAF to be awarded the Medal of Honor.

15 September–28 October: The first contingent of 27th Fighter Escort Wing F–84E Thunderjet fighters leaves Bergstrom AFB, Texas, on 15 September, arriving in West Germany on 18 September. The second contingent leaves Texas on 15 October, arriving in West Germany on 28 October. The 27th Fighter Escort Wing receives the Mackay Trophy for this flight.

22 September: Col David C. Schilling completes the first nonstop flight over the Atlantic by a jet aircraft, landing his F–84 Thunderjet at Limestone, Maine, after flying 3,300 miles from England in ten hours, one minute.

28 September: Eight white mice survive a flight to an altitude of 97,000 feet in a balloon launched at Holloman AFB, New Mexico.

29 September: The USAF announces that a parachute jump of 42,449 feet was made by Capt Richard V. Wheeler at Holloman AFB.

8 November: In history's first battle between jet aircraft, a USAF F–80 Shooting Star, piloted by Lt Russell J. Brown, downs a North Korean MiG–15.

29 November–8 December: Combat Cargo Command mounts a maximum effort to supply the 1st Marine Division trapped by Chinese forces at the Chosin Reservoir. Altogether, C–119s and C–47s air-drop or land on rough air strips 1,580 tons of supplies and equipment, including eight bridge spans, and evacuate almost 5,000 sick and wounded marines.

5 December: Combat Cargo Command uses 131 flights to evacuate 3,925 patients from Korea. This is the Korean War's largest day of aeromedical airlift.

14–17 December: Combat Cargo Command evacuates 228 patients, 3,891 other passengers, and 20,088 tons of cargo from Yonpo Airfield as Chinese troops press the X Corps in the Hamhung-Hungnam defense perimeter. Naval transports remove the remainder of X Corps by 24 December.

1951

15–16 February: H–5 helicopter pilots of the 3d Air Rescue Squadron brave a blinding snowstorm and 40-knot winds to deliver blood plasma and medical supplies to the U.S. Army 2d Division at Chipyong, Korea, and to evacuate 52 wounded men.

1 March: The USAF establishes its northernmost operational base, Thule AB, Greenland, 690 miles north of the Arctic Circle.

15 March: A Boeing KC–97A Stratofreighter tanker success-fully refuels a B–47 jet bomber in-flight.

18 April: An Aerobee research rocket flies a monkey into space, the first primate in space, from Holloman AFB.

20 May: Capt James Jabara becomes the world's first jet ace, shooting down his fifth and sixth MiGs in the Korean War.

6 July: An Air Materiel Command KB–29M tanker, operated by a SAC crew assigned to the 43d Air Refueling Squadron, conducts the first air refueling over enemy territory under combat conditions. The tanker refuels four RF–80 Shooting Stars flying reconnaissance missions over North Korea.

17 August: Flying a combat-equipped F-86E Sabrejet, Col Fred J. Ascani sets a world-speed record of 635.6 mph in the 100-kilometer closed-course competition at the National Air Races in Detroit, Michigan. Colonel Ascani will receive the Mackay Trophy for the meritorious flight of 1951.

24 August: Air Force Chief of Staff Gen Hoyt S. Vandenberg reports that the February 1951 Nevada atomic bomb tests evaluated a new atomic tactical weapon for use against armies in the field.

13 September: The USAF announces establishment of its first pilotless bomber squadron at Missile Test Center, Cocoa, Florida.

14 September: Capt John S. Walmsley Jr., USAF, loses his life illuminating an enemy supply train while piloting a searchlight-equipped B–26 Invader. Disabling the enemy train with bombs, Captain Walmsley makes repeated passes over the halted train, taking no evasive action, to guide other USAF aircraft to the target. He earns the Medal of Honor.

20 September: The USAF makes the first successful recovery of animals from a rocket flight when a monkey and 11 mice survive an Aerobee flight to an altitude of 236,000 feet.

23 October: The 306th Bombardment Wing, Medium, receives the first production B–47 Stratojet medium bomber to enter service. This aircraft will become the workhorse of SAC through most of the 1950s.

1952

7 January: The USAF announces plans to increase its effective combat strength by 50 percent and personnel by 20 percent. The result will be a full 143-wing, 1,273,200-person Air Force.

8 January: Exercise Snowfall begins the largest U.S. airlift of troops to date. During 8–13 January, approximately 100 planes of the 516th Troop Carrier Wing airlift 8,623 troops from Fort Campbell, Kentucky, to Wheeler-Sack Army Air Field, New York.

1 February: The U.S. Air Force acquires its first general-purpose, high-speed digital computer, a vacuum-tube-based Univac I.

F–86 Sabres enabled American pilots to turn the tide of the air war in Korea in favor of the Allies.

10 February: Leading a flight of three F–86 Sabrejets on a combat air patrol mission near the Manchurian border, Maj George A. Davis Jr. engages 12 enemy MiG–15 jet fighters in aerial combat. After shooting down two enemy aircraft and completely disrupting the enemy formation, Major Davis is himself shot down and killed. Major Davis is the first USAF member to become an ace in two wars, World War II and Korea. He earns the Medal of Honor for his sacrifice.

15 April: The YB–52, eight-jet Stratofortress prototype, the first all-jet intercontinental heavy bomber, makes its first flight.

3 May: A ski-and-wheel-equipped USAF C–47 Skytrain makes the world's first successful North Pole landing.

23–24 June: Combined air elements of the U.S. Air Force, Navy, and Marine Corps virtually destroy the electric power potential of North Korea. The two-day attack, involving over 1,200 sorties, is the largest single air effort since World War II.

2 July: The USAF discloses a new jet fighter, the Lockheed F–94C Starfire, the first Air Force fighter armed solely with rockets.

14 July: The Ground Observer Corps initiates the 24-hour-a-day Skywatch program as part of a nationwide air-defense effort.

17 July: Fifty-eight F–84 Thunderjets of 31st Fighter Escort Wing complete a record transoceanic mass-jet flight. The flight, under Col David C. Schilling, left Turner AFB, Georgia, on 4 July, and landed at Yokota AB, Japan, on 16 and 17 July, flying 10,895 miles with seven stops and two aerial refuelings. This is the first mass-fighter deployment supported by in-flight refueling.

19 July: The USAF announces the first successful flying of balloons at controlled constant stratospheric altitudes for periods lasting over three days.

29 July: An RB–45 assigned to the 91st Strategic Reconnaissance Wing flies from Elmendorf AFB, Alaska, to Yokota AB making the first nonstop transpacific flight by a jet aircraft. Maj Louis H. Carrington Jr., Maj Frederick W. Shook, and

Capt Wallace D. Yancey earn the 1952 Mackay Trophy for this flight.

31 July: Two USAF MATS Sikorsky H–19 helicopters complete the first transatlantic helicopter flight, having flown in five stages from Westover Field, Massachusetts, to Prestwick, Scotland.

30 September: The Bell Rascal GAM–63 air-to-surface strategic missile launches for the first time.

22 November: While leading a flight of four F–80 Shooting Star fighters dive-bombing enemy gun positions, Maj Charles J. Loring deliberately crashes his damaged aircraft into enemy emplacements. Major Loring earns the Medal of Honor for his sacrifice.

26 November: A Northrop B–62 Snark, a turbojet-powered subsonic long-range missile, is launched for the first time from a zero-length launcher.

1953

8 February: The American Medical Association recognizes Aviation Medicine as a medical specialty, the first one to evolve from military practice and research.

25 May: George Welch, North American test pilot, flies the prototype YF–100 Super Sabre for the first time, taking off and landing at Air Force Flight Test Center, Edwards AFB, California.

8 June: At Luke AFB, Arizona, the USAF Thunderbirds, officially designated the 3600th Air Demonstration Flight, perform for the first time.

11 July: Maj John F. Bolt becomes the first jet ace in Marine Corps history while flying the F–86 Sabrejet on temporary duty with the Air Force's 51st Fighter Interceptor Wing.

27 July: Capt Ralph S. Parr Jr. gains the last aerial victory of the Korean War by shooting down an Il-2 at 12:30 P.M. The armistice became effective at 10:01 P.M.

20 August: During Operation Longstride, F–84 Thunderjets assigned to the 31st Strategic Fighter Wing fly from Albany, Georgia, to Nouasseur AB, Morocco. On the same day 17 F–84G Thunderjets assigned to the 508th Strategic Fighter Wing fly nonstop 4,485 miles from Albany to Lakenheath, England. These first nonstop transatlantic flights by fighters demonstrate SAC's capability for rapid long-range deployment and earn the Mackay Trophy.

25 August: The USAF announces that it has transformed a B–36 Peacemaker bomber into a "flying aircraft carrier" capable of launching and recovering an F–84 Thunderjet fighter in flight.

1 September: The USAF announces the first instance of aerial refueling of jet-powered aircraft by jet-powered aircraft, in which a standard B–47 Stratojet received fuel in the air from a KB–47B Stratojet.

11 September: The Sidewinder infrared-guided air-to-air missile makes the first successful interception, sending an F–6F drone down in flames.

14 October: The X–10, prototype of the North American B–64 Navaho ramjet-propelled surface-to-surface guided missile, makes initial flight.

12 December: Maj Charles E. Yeager, USAF, attains speed of 1,650 mph—about twice that of sound—at Edwards AFB in a Bell X–1A rocket ship launched from a B–36 bomber.

1954

24 February: President Dwight D. Eisenhower approves a National Security Council recommendation for construction of a distant early warning line.

1 March: The United States explodes the first hydrogen bomb in the Marshall Islands.

16 March: Representative W. Sterling Cole, chairman of the Joint Atomic Energy Committee, reports that the United States has a hydrogen weapon that can be delivered by airplane to any target in the world.

1 April: President Eisenhower signs into law a bill creating the Air Force Academy.

24 June: Secretary of the Air Force Harold E. Talbott announces the permanent location of the Air Force Academy will be a 15,000-acre tract of land six miles north of Colorado Springs, Colorado.

15 July: The first jet-powered transport built in the U.S., the Boeing 707, flight-tests near Seattle, Washington. This aircraft is the prototype for military Stratotanker and commercial Stratoliner.

26 July: Lt Gen Hubert R. Harmon is appointed the first superintendent of the Air Force Academy.

6–7 August: Two B–47 Stratojets assigned to the 308th Bombardment Wing fly a 10,000-mile nonstop flight from Hunter AFB, Georgia, to French Morocco and back to Hunter AFB. The 308th Bombardment Wing wins the Mackay Trophy for this flight. During the same period, two B–47 Stratojet wings assigned to the 38th Air Division depart Hunter AFB, fly a simulated bombing mission, and recover in French Morocco, demonstrating the ability of strategic bombers to operate from forward bases.

1 November: The USAF B–29 Superfortress, the aircraft famed for having dropped atom bombs on Hiroshima and Nagasaki, Japan, is withdrawn from service.

2 November: Test pilot J. F. Coleman, flying Convair XYF–1, takes off in vertical flight, shifts to horizontal, and changes back to vertical for landing at San Diego, California.

7 December: The USAF makes the first successful recovery of a missile, a Navaho X–10, using a fully automatic approach and landing system at Edwards AFB.

10 December: In a rocket-propelled sled run, Col John P. Stapp, USAF, attains speed of 632 mph and sustains greater G-force than ever endured in recorded deceleration tests—the equivalent of Mach 1.7 at 35,000 feet. The test determines that humans can survive ejection from aircraft at supersonic speeds.

1955

6 April: A missile launched by a B–36 Peacemaker bomber at a height of 42,000 feet explodes its nuclear warhead some six miles above Yucca Flat, Nevada. This is the highest known altitude of any nuclear blast.

29 June: The first Boeing B–52 Stratofortress to enter USAF operational service is delivered to the 93d Bombardment Wing, Castle AFB, California.

July: The Air Force Academy admits its first class of 306 cadets at Lowery AFB, Colorado, its temporary location until it can move to Colorado Springs.

20 August: Col Horace A. Hanes, USAF, flying an F-100 Super Sabre over the Mojave Desert, establishes a new speed record of 822.135 mph. Colonel Hanes, the director of Flight Testing, Air Force Flight Test Center, Edwards AFB, will receive the Mackay Trophy for his record-breaking flight.

6 October: DOD announces that it has awarded a contract to Glenn L. Martin Company as primary contractor for building a rocket vehicle for launching an earth satellite. Martin receives authorization to contract with General Electric Company for construction of the rocket motor for the launching vehicle.

22 October: The Republic F–105A Thunderchief fighter-bomber, designed to carry nuclear weapons and support field armies, exceeds the speed of sound on its initial flight at Edwards AFB.

1956

17 January: DOD reveals the existence of semiautomatic ground environment (SAGE), an automated electronic air-defense system. SAGE radars transmit data rapidly via telephone lines to direction/combat centers where large computers process the information.

21 May: At an altitude of 50,000 feet over the Pacific, Maj David Crichlow, USAF, in a B–52 Stratofortress bomber, drops the first airborne hydrogen bomb, which explodes on Bikini Atoll.

7 September: Capt Iven C. Kincheloe Jr. sets the altitude record for manned flight at Edwards AFB piloting a Bell X–2 transonic rocket-powered aircraft to a height of 126,200 feet. Captain Kincheloe receives the Mackay Trophy for this flight.

15 September: The 701st Tactical Missile Wing (TMW), scheduled to be equipped with the Matador cruise missile, activates under Twelfth Air Force at Hahn AB, Germany. This is the first USAF TMW.

27 September: An X–2 transonic rocket-powered plane, piloted by Capt Milburn G. Apt and launched from a B–50 bomber, sets a speed record of 2,094 mph over the Mojave Desert. Later in the flight the aircraft crashes, killing the pilot.

11 November: USAF's first supersonic bomber, the delta-wing Convair B–58 Hustler, capable of flying at a speed of 1,000 mph, makes its initial flight at Fort Worth, Texas.

26 November: Secretary of Defense Charles E. Wilson issues a memorandum to the Armed Forces Policy Council establishing the areas of jurisdiction of three U.S. armed services in developing missiles of various ranges. Secretary Wilson gives the USAF operational jurisdiction over long-range missiles.

30 November: A Martin TM–61 Matador, a jet-propelled missile, completes its final test flight and becomes USAF's first operational tactical missile. With a range of several hundred miles, the Matador cruises at 650 mph and has a ceiling of 35,000 feet.

9 December: The 463d Troop Carrier Wing receives USAF's first C–130 Hercules tactical cargo and troop carrier. This four-engined turboprop airlifter has an unrefueled range of over 2,500 miles. It can carry outsized cargo of almost 50,000 pounds or up to 92 troops, and can take off and land within about 3,600 feet.

CHRONOLOGY
1957—1966

1957

18 January: Commanded by Maj Gen Archie J. Old Jr., USAF, three B–52 Stratofortresses complete a 24,325-mile around-the-world nonstop flight, nicknamed Operation Power Flite, in 45 hours, 19 minutes, and an average speed of 534 mph. The 93d Strategic Bombardment Wing wins the Mackay Trophy for this first globe-circling, nonstop flight by jet aircraft.

12 April: The USAF discloses the Ryan X–13 Vertijet research plane, capable of vertical takeoff and landings, has flown successfully at Edwards AFB.

19 April: A Douglas Thor (XSM–75) intermediate-range ballistic missile successfully launches at Cape Canaveral.

2 June: Capt Joseph W. Kittinger Jr., USAF, establishes the altitude-endurance record for manned lighter-than-air aircraft by remaining aloft in a balloon over Minnesota for six hours, 34 minutes. Two hours of that time was spent above 96,000 feet.

11 June: Assigned to the 4080th Strategic Reconnaissance Wing, the first U–2 high-altitude, long-range reconnaissance aircraft arrives at Laughlin AFB, Texas. The U–2 can fly ten-hour missions at exceptionally high altitudes at a top speed of 600 mph.

28 June: Assigned to the 93d Air Refueling Squadron, the first KC–135 Stratotanker arrives at Castle AFB. The jet tanker can cruise at the same speed as jet bombers while refueling, drastically reducing the time for missions requiring in-flight refueling.

1 July: The 704th Strategic Missile Wing (SMW) activates at Cooke AFB, California. This is the first USAF ICBM wing.

19 July: The USAF fires the first air-to-air nuclear defense rocket, the Douglas MB–1 Genie, from an F–89J over Yucca Flat, Nevada.

31 July: The distant early warning line, a string of early warning radar installations extending across the Canadian Arctic, is declared fully operational.

Atlas, the free world's first intercontinental ballistic missile, had a range of more than 5,500 nautical miles.

1 August: The North American Air Defense Command, a joint United States-Canadian command with an air-defense mission, is informally established.

15 August: Gen Nathan F. Twining becomes the first USAF officer to serve as chairman of the Joint Chiefs of Staff.

20 September: The USAF chief of staff, Gen Thomas D. White, announces development of radar units capable of detecting ICBMs at distances of 3,000 miles.

4 October: The Soviet Union launches *Sputnik*, the world's first artificial space satellite.

11 October: A Thor intermediate-range ballistic missile is launched at Cape Canaveral, exceeding its designed 1,500-mile range and landing in the Atlantic Ocean 2,000 miles from launching point. It is the second Thor to be successfully tested.

16 October: The USAF successfully launches an Aerobee rocket to a height of 35 miles, where its nose cone separates and travels to a height of 54 miles. At this point, shaped charges blast pellets into space at a speed of 33,000 mph, surpassing by 8,000 mph the speed necessary to escape from the earth's gravity.

22 October: Operation Far Side, a four-stage rocket, fires from a balloon at 100,000 feet above Eniwetok, penetrating at least 2,700 miles into outer space.

21 November: DOD announces that the first ICBM base will be built at Francis E. Warren AFB, Wyoming.

29 November: Gen Thomas D. White announces the assignment of the intercontinental and intermediate-range ballistic missile programs to SAC as well as the transfer of the 1st Missile Division to SAC, and that the San Bernardino Air Force Depot will support the long-range ballistic missile program.

15 December: The 556th Strategic Missile Squadron (SMS), the first SM–62 Snark operational squadron, activates at Patrick AFB, Florida.

17 December: USAF accomplishes its first successful firing of an Atlas intercontinental ballistic missile (ICBM). The Atlas reentry vehicle lands in the target area after a flight of 500 miles.

19 December: The fourth successfully tested Thor missile completes the first fully guided intermediate-range ballistic missile flight using an all-inertial guidance system.

1958

1 January: The USAF activates the 672d Strategic Missile Squadron, with Thor intermediate-range ballistic missile, at Cooke (later, Vandenberg) AFB with Col Harry H. Zink as commander.

15 January: The USAF activates the 475th Air Defense Missile Wing and assigns it the mission of developing and conducting a training program for Bomarc missile units. The Bomarc is an unmanned supersonic interceptor capable of destroying targets at ranges between 250 and 450 nautical miles.

31 January: Explorer I, the first U.S. satellite to go into orbit, is launched by a Jupiter C rocket from Cape Canaveral.

8 February: The USAF institutes systems management of a ballistic early warning system when it contracts with RCA to manage existing communications facilities, including the distant early warning line and SAGE systems, designed to provide maximum early warning to the North American Air Defense Command, SAC, and civil defense agencies.

27 February: Missile Director William M. Holaday approves USAF's Minuteman Project, a program for building 5,000-mile-range solid-fuel ballistic missiles launched from underground installations.

17 March: Vanguard I, second U.S. satellite to go into orbit, is launched from Cape Canaveral.

28 April: After an in-flight explosion, the pilot and navigator of a 341st Bombardment Wing B-47 eject successfully. While attempting to egress, the copilot, 1st Lt James E. Obenauf, notices another crew member unconscious and incapable of escape. Instead of ejecting, Lieutenant Obenauf remains on the crippled and burning aircraft, piloting it from the backseat position to a safe landing at Dyess AFB, Texas. He will receive the Distinguished Flying Cross for his heroism.

27 June: At Cape Canaveral the 556th Strategic Missile Squadron successfully completes the first military launching of a Snark intercontinental cruise missile.

9 July: A USAF Thor-Able reentry test vehicle, in the first nose cone test at ICBM range and velocity, carries a mouse some 6,000 miles over the Atlantic Ocean in flight from Cape Canaveral to the Ascension Island area.

15 July: After Lebanon asks the U.S. for assistance, Tactical Air Command (TAC) dispatches Composite Air Strike Force Bravo to the Middle East in 12 hours.

1 August: A missile-borne nuclear weapon detonates at high altitude over Johnston Island in the Pacific as part of a program to develop an anti-ICBM defense.

28 August: Cape Canaveral launches an Atlas ICBM that accurately flies a 3,000-mile course and lands in the target area in the first test of radio-command guidance system.

September: Responding to Chinese communist threats to the Taiwan Straits, a TAC Composite Strike Force (that includes F–100 Super Sabres, F–101 Voodoos, B–57 Canberras, and C–130 Hercules) deploys to the Far East. Its rapid and effective deployment wins the Mackay Trophy.

24 September: A Bomarc missile pilotless interceptor launches from Cape Canaveral by a semiautomatic ground-environment unit in Kingston, New York, destroying a 1,000-mph target flying 48,000 feet over the Atlantic Ocean at a distance of 75 miles.

1 October: The National Aeronautics and Space Administration (NASA) is established to control nonmilitary scientific space projects.

11 October: A USAF-launched Pioneer I lunar probe vehicle attains a height of approximately 80,000 miles before falling back to the earth on 13 October.

16 December: The Pacific Missile Range begins launching operations with the successful flight of a Thor missile, the first ballistic missile launched over the Pacific Ocean.

18 December: The USAF places in orbit the first artificial communications satellite, a Project Score relay vehicle integral with the four-ton Atlas launcher. The next day, the satellite broadcasts a taped recording of President Dwight D. Eisenhower's Christmas message.

1959

15 January: SAC orders the first integration of missile and bomber forces by transferring the 703d Strategic Missile Wing (ICBM Titan) and the 706th Strategic Missile Wing (ICBM Atlas) from 1st Missile Division to Fifteenth Air Force.

21 January: The U.S. Army's first tactical Jupiter intermediate-range ballistic missile strikes target area after a 1,700-mile flight test. The Jupiter will eventually become a USAF weapon system.

1 February: Operational control of the distant early warning line is transferred from USAF to Royal Canadian Air Force.

6 February: The USAF successfully launches the first Titan I ICBM. With a range of 5,500 nautical miles, the two-stage liquid-fueled missile will be deployed in underground silos but has to be raised to the surface before launch.

12 February: SAC retires its last B-36 Peacemaker to become an all-jet bomber force.

28 February: The USAF successfully launches the *Discoverer I* satellite into polar orbit from Vandenberg AFB, California.

6 April: NASA announces that seven pilots from U.S. armed services are chosen for the Mercury astronaut program established to train the first U.S. space pilot. Among those selected are USAF Capts L. Gordon Cooper Jr., Virgil I. "Gus" Grissom, and Donald K. "Deke" Slayton.

23 April: The GAM–77 Hound Dog supersonic missile designed to deliver a nuclear warhead over a distance of several hundred miles test-fires for the first time from a B–52 bomber at Eglin AFB, Florida.

28 May: Monkeys Able and Baker are recovered alive from the Atlantic Ocean near Antigua Island after a flight to an altitude of 300 miles in the nose cone of a Jupiter missile launched from Cape Canaveral.

3 June: The Air Force Academy graduates the first class of 207 graduates. Two hundred and five receive commissions as regular officers in USAF.

8 June: Piloted by Scott Crossfield, the seven and one-half-ton X–15 hypersonic rocket plane, designed for speeds up to 4,000 mph and altitudes to 100 miles, drops from a B–52 more than seven miles above the Mojave Desert for a nonpowered glide test—its first free flight.

7 August: Two USAF F–100s make the first flight by jet fighter aircraft over the North Pole.

9 September: A SAC crew fires an Atlas ICBM for the first time from Vandenberg AFB. The missile travels 4,300 miles at 16,000 mph. After this shot, SAC's commander in chief declares Atlas operational

1 October: The USAF Aerospace Medical Center activates at Brooks AFB, Texas, absorbing the former School of Aviation Medicine, the USAF Hospital at Lackland AFB, Texas, and other facilities.

28 October–19 December: The 4520th Aerial Demonstration Team, better known as the Thunderbirds, tours the Far East, earning the Mackay Trophy.

31 October: A Series D Atlas ICBM goes on alert at Vandenberg AFB. This is the first American ICBM equipped with a nuclear warhead to be placed on alert status.

1960

May: SAC places one-third of its bombers and tankers on 15-minute ground alert.

A three-man aircrew scrambles for its B–58 Hustler. The delta-wing aircraft was well named since it could fly at twice the speed of sound.

1 August: SAC's 43d Bombardment Wing at Carswell AFB accepts the first operational B-58 Hustler medium bomber. The United States's first supersonic bomber, the delta-wing aircraft flies at twice the speed of sound and can be refueled in-flight.

11 August: Recovery of a 300-pound capsule ejected by USAF's *Discoverer XIII* marks the first recovery of an object ejected by an orbiting satellite. Planned aerial retrieval is abandoned when the capsule lands outside the designated area; recovery is made by U.S. Navy frogmen.

19 August: Piloting a C–119, Capt Harold F. Mitchell, USAF, retrieves the *Discoverer XIV* reentry capsule in midair. This is the first successful aerial recovery of a returning space capsule. The 6593d Test Squadron (Special) wins the Mackay Trophy for the aerial recovery of reentry vehicles.

30 August: With six Atlas missiles ready to launch, the 564th Strategic Missile Squadron at Francis E. Warren AFB becomes the first fully operational ICBM squadron.

19 December: In an unmanned test of the Mercury space capsule, NASA uses a Redstone rocket booster to launch the capsule from Cape Canaveral. The vehicle attains a speed of 4,200 mph, a height of 135 miles, and a distance of 235 miles. Landing safely by parachute, it is recovered within 32 minutes.

1961

31 January: A Redstone booster carrying Ham, a chimpanzee, in a Mercury space capsule launches from Cape Canaveral on an 18-minute, 420-mile flight. Ham performs well during the flight, apparently suffering no ill-effects.

1 February: The ballistic missile early warning system (BMEWS) site at Thule, Greenland, becomes operational. Subsequently, other sites become operational at Clear, Alaska, and Fylingdales in the United Kingdom. Operated by the North American Air Defense Command, the BMEWS provides SAC with sufficient warning of an impending missile or aircraft attack to launch its own alert force.

1 February: A Minuteman ICBM launches for the first time at Cape Canaveral in a major test. Under full guidance, the solid-fueled missile travels 4,600 miles, hitting the target area.

3 February: SAC initiates the Looking Glass airborne command post. Maintaining continuous 24-hour coverage in shifts, Looking Glass aircraft are converted KC–135 Stratotankers equipped to communicate with the Joint Chiefs of Staff, any SAC base, or any SAC aircraft in the air or on the ground.

13 February: The USAF successfully launches its new solid-fueled, air-to-surface missile, GAM–83B Bullpup, at supersonic speed from an F–100 Super Sabre. A modified version of a U.S. Navy missile, GAM–83B can carry a nuclear weapon. The pilot of the parent airplane can guide it to target.

7 March: SAC declares operational the Quail, a diversionary missile (GAM–72A) to be used with the B–52.

17 April: A constant-altitude balloon, launched at Vernalis, California, by USAF's Cambridge Research Center, remains at 70,000 feet for nine days with a 40-pound payload.

3 May: An Air Force Systems Command (AFSC) crew launches a Titan I ICBM from a hard "silo lift" launcher for the first time at Vandenberg AFB.

26 May: A B–58 Hustler supersonic bomber from the 43d Bombardment Wing sets a record flying from New York to Paris in three hours, 19 minutes, 41 seconds at an average speed of 1,302 mph. The crew, consisting of Maj William R. Payne, Capt William L. Polhemus, and Capt Raymond Wagener, win the Mackay Trophy for the flight.

1 June: At Kincheloe AFB, Michigan, the first Bomarc–B pilotless interceptor site is declared operational.

9 June: Delivery of the first C–135 Stratolifter jet cargo aircraft marks the beginning of modernization of MATS's former all-propeller-driven fleet.

July: SAC places 50 percent of its bombers and tankers on 15-minute ground alert.

1 July: The North American Air Defense Command begins operation of a space detection and tracking system designed to provide electronic cataloging of man-made space objects.

21 July: America's second Project Mercury astronaut, Capt Virgil I. Grissom, USAF, attains an altitude of 118 miles and a speed of 5,310 mph in a 303-mile suborbital space flight from Cape Canaveral in the *Liberty Bell 7* capsule launched by a Mercury-Redstone 4 booster.

8 August: The USAF launches an Atlas F missile from Cape Canaveral for the first time. The Atlas F, designed for long-term storage of liquid fuels and for shortened countdown, is the only Atlas model destined for emplacement in hardened underground silos.

13 September: The world-wide Mercury tracking network is used for the first time in observing the orbit of an unmanned Mercury vehicle. The test convinces NASA that the Atlas vehicle is capable of launching a man into orbit.

19 September: The SAGE Center at Gunter AFB, Alabama, controls the flight of a Bomarc B pilotless interceptor from launch at Eglin AFB to interception of a Regulus II supersonic drone at an altitude of seven miles and distance of 250 miles off the Florida coast. The missile successfully makes a U-turn maneuver.

9 November: Maj Robert M. White, USAF, attains a top speed of 4,093 mph in an X–15 hypersonic rocket plane while flying at full throttle at an altitude of 101,600 feet.

17 November: The USAF successfully launches the first Minuteman intercontinental missile from an underground silo at Cape Canaveral. It flies 3,000 miles down the Atlantic Missile Range.

29 November: NASA's Mercury vehicle, containing two chimpanzees, successfully completes a two-orbit flight around the earth after launch from Cape Canaveral.

1 December: The first Minuteman Missile Squadron, the 10th Strategic Missile Squadron, is activated at Malmstrom AFB, Montana.

15 December: The North American Air Defense Command's SAGE system becomes fully operational with completion of its 21st and last control center at Sioux City, Iowa.

1962

29 January: The last Titan I test-fires from Cape Canaveral on a 5,000-mile flight. Of 47 shots, 34 are successful, nine partially successful, and four unsuccessful.

2 February: A USAF C–123 Provider aircraft crashes in South Vietnam while spraying defoliant during Operation Ranch Hand. This is the first USAF aircraft loss in South Vietnam.

5 March: The crew of a B–58 Hustler bomber assigned to the 43d Bombardment Wing sets three speed records in a round-trip flight between New York City and Los Angeles,

Artist's conception of the hypersonic X–15 rocket plane as it is released into flight from its mount below the wing of a B–52.

California. The Hustler makes the trip in four hours, 41 minutes, 15 seconds, averaging 1,044.46 mph. The crew receives the Mackay Trophy for this flight.

21 March: A bear becomes the first living creature ejected from a supersonic aircraft when the USAF tests an escape capsule designed for installation in the B–58. Ejecting at 35,000 feet from a B–58 flying 870 mph, the bear lands unharmed seven minutes, 49 seconds later.

18 April: At Lowry AFB SAC declares operational the USAF's first Titan I squadron, the 724th Strategic Missile Squadron, equipped with nine missiles, the first emplaced in hardened, underground installations.

19 June: Astronaut Capt Virgil I. Grissom, USAF, receives the first Gen Thomas D. White USAF Space Trophy from Secretary of the Air Force Eugene M. Zuckert for his "outstanding contribution to the nation's progress in aerospace in Mercury spacecraft *Liberty Bell 7* flight."

29 June: A USAF team fires the first Minuteman from an underground silo at Cape Canaveral to a target area 2,300 miles downrange. This is the first Minuteman launched by a military crew.

8 July: A Thor rocket carries a megaton-plus hydrogen device to an altitude above 200 miles in a launch from Johnston Island in Operation Dominic. The detonation of the nuclear device at that altitude marks the highest U.S. thermonuclear blast.

17 July: Maj Robert M. White, USAF, pilots the X–15–1 hypersonic experimental aircraft to a world-record altitude of 58.7 miles during which the X–15 achieves its original design altitude. Maximum speed is 3,784 mph.

19 July: A Nike-Zeus antimissile missile fired from Kwajalein Island makes the first known interception of an ICBM when it brings down the nose cone of an Atlas missile launched from Vandenberg AFB.

1 August: The USAF launches the first Atlas F from an underground silo on a successful 5,000-mile flight from Vandenberg AFB to the Pacific Test Range in the vicinity of the Marshall Islands.

9 August: The USAF gives the first U.S. demonstration of multiple-countdown capability by launching two Atlas D missiles in rapid succession from Cape Canaveral on 5,000-mile flights.

14 October: A U.S. Air Force reconnaissance flight proves the existence of Russian missile sites in Cuba.

27 October: A 4080th Strategic Wing U–2 reconnaissance aircraft piloted by Maj Rudolf Anderson Jr. is shot down over Cuba. Lost with his aircraft, Major Anderson posthumously receives the first Air Force Cross for his sacrifice.

27 October: SAC places on alert the first ten Minuteman I ICBMs, assigned to the 10th SMS, 341st Missile Wing, Malmstrom AFB.

5 December: The USAF completes the Atlas flight-test program with launch of an "F" model from Cape Canaveral on a 5,000-mile flight. Of 151 missiles launched, 108 make successful flights.

11 December: SAC declares fully operational two flights of Minuteman I ICBMs assigned to the 10th Strategic Missile Squadron, Malmstrom AFB.

13–14 December: The USAF's Project Stargazer balloon, manned by Capt Joseph A. Kittinger Jr., USAF, and William C. White, U.S. Navy civilian astronomer, reach an altitude of 82,000 feet in an 18.5-hour flight over southwestern New Mexico. A telescope mounted atop the gondola gives White the clearest celestial view ever experienced by an astronomer.

22 December: A U.S. Army Nike-Zeus antimissile missile fired from Kwajalein Island intercepts an Atlas launched on a 4,800-mile flight from Vandenberg AFB, demonstrating for the first time the ability of a Nike-Zeus to discriminate between an intended target and accompanying decoys.

1963

6 February: The 655th Aerospace Test Wing crew becomes the first USAF unit to launch a Titan II missile in a firing from Cape Canaveral.

1 March: The USAF achieves its first successful launch of an advanced ballistic reentry system in a firing from Cape Canaveral.

7 May: Dr. Theodore von Karman, distinguished U.S. physicist, dies in Aachen, West Germany, a few days before his 82d birthday.

15 May: Astronaut Maj L. Gordon Cooper Jr., USAF, launches from Cape Canaveral in Project Mercury capsule *Faith 7*. On 16 May, after completing 22 orbits of earth in 34 hours, 19 minutes, 49 seconds, he lands in the Pacific about 60 miles southeast of Midway Island. He is the first American to orbit the earth for more than one day and the last pilot of the Project Mercury series.

8 June: The 570th Strategic Missile Squadron, the first Titan II ICBM squadron to be operational, activates at Davis-Monthan AFB, Arizona, and is assigned to SAC.

20 July: The crew members of C–47 *Extol Pink* distinguish themselves in evacuating wounded Vietnamese at night under heavy enemy fire. Capts Warren P. Tomsett, John R. Ordemann, and Donald R. Mack; TSgt Edsol P. Inlow; and SSgts Jack E. Morgan and Frank C. Barrett win the Mackay Trophy for this deed.

1 August: NASA's Mariner II, launched by USAF on 27 August 1962 from Cape Canaveral, completes its first orbit around the sun. It traveled approximately 540 million miles to complete the first solar orbit.

10 October: Seven original members of the Project Mercury astronaut team receive the Collier Trophy.

16 October: At Cape Canaveral the U.S. Air Force inaugurates a space-based nuclear detection system by launching twin satellites designed to assume circular 7,000-mile-high orbits on opposite sides of the earth. The 475-pound, 20-sided satellites, known as Project Vela Hotel or Project 823, are designed to detect nuclear explosions.

29 November: By executive order, President Lyndon B. Johnson renames Cape Canaveral as Cape Kennedy and redesignates space facilities there as the John F. Kennedy Space Center.

17 December: USAF's new C–141A Starlifter jet cargo transport flies for the first time at Dobbins AFB, Georgia. Capable of crossing any ocean nonstop at more than 500 mph, the Starlifter can transport 154 troops, 123 paratroopers, or a combination of men and supplies. It can carry a 70,000-pound payload.

1964

8 April: The USAF's Titan II launch booster blasts into orbit the first Gemini spacecraft. The Gemini series comprises the first U.S.-manned orbital spacecraft.

21 April: The number of SAC ICBMs on alert equals the number of bombers on ground alert. From this day forward, the share of nuclear deterrence shouldered by the missile force will gradually outstrip that shouldered by the main bomber force.

11 May: The USAF's XB–70 Valkyrie, built by North American Aviation, rolls out at Palmdale, California. Designed to fly three times the speed of sound and at altitudes above 70,000 feet, the 275-ton aircraft measures 185 feet in length and 105 feet in wing span.

27 July: The 1964 Daniel Guggenheim Medal is awarded posthumously to Dr. Robert H. Goddard, the pioneer rocket scientist.

28 July: NASA's Ranger VII spacecraft launches from Cape Kennedy on a flight to the moon. On 31 July Ranger VII will complete its mission of taking and relaying 4,316 high-quality close-up pictures of the lunar surface before crashing into an area northwest of the Sea of Clouds.

19 August: Syncom III communications satellite is launched by Thor-Delta launch vehicle. By 23 September after several weeks of minor maneuvers, it will achieve almost perfect stationary position (apogee 22,311 miles, perigee 22,164 miles) above the equator and international date line. For 15 days from 7 October, it will transmit the Olympic Games from Tokyo, Japan. It is the world's first geostationary satellite.

1 September: USAF Capts Albert R. Crews and Richard E. Lawler complete a two-week stay in a simulated space cabin at General Electric Space Center, Valley Forge, Pennsylvania. According to officials, the test demonstrates that man can perform more tasks in extended space flight than previously assumed.

11 September: The USAF announces the retirement of two squadrons of Atlas ICBMs and impending retirement of 105 more liquid-fueled missiles made obsolete by the solid-fueled Minuteman.

17 September: President Johnson announces that the United States is installing recently developed, over-the-horizon-type radar capable of "seeing" around the curvature of the earth and of detecting a missile shortly after its launch.

21 September: At Palmdale, California, the B–70A Valkyrie flies for the first time.

17–26 November: C–130 Hercules aircrews of the 464th Troop Carrier Wing carry Belgiam paratroopers to deal with unrest in Zaire, the former Belgiam Congo, airlifting refugees to France on return flights. The airlift is instrumental in saving the lives of nearly 2,000 hostages and wins the Mackay Trophy.

21 December: A USAF F–111A (later nicknamed Aardvark) variable-sweep-wing fighter makes a successful maiden flight at Carswell AFB.

22 December: President Johnson approves the inclusion in fiscal year (FY) 1966 budget of funds for development of the C–5A transport, later nicknamed Galaxy. The new aircraft can carry 345 troops or up to 250,000 pounds of cargo to 6,500 miles, without refueling, at a speed of approximately 550 mph.

22 December: The new USAF strategic reconnaissance plane, the SR–71 Blackbird, in its first flight at Palmdale exceeds an altitude of 45,000 feet and speed of 1,000 mph. The USAF team that tested the SR-71 will receive the Mackay Trophy.

1965

1 January: The USAF's first SR–71 Blackbird unit, the 4200th Strategic Reconnaissance Wing, activates at Beale AFB, California.

18 January: The short-range attack missile program is announced by the President in his defense message to Congress. Launched from a B–52 Stratofortress or FB–111 Aardvark, the nuclear-tipped missile can hit targets 50 nautical miles from the aircraft.

21 January: The Air Force Cambridge Research Laboratories, Office of Aerospace Research, Hanscom AFB, Massachusetts, "bounces" a laser beam off the Explorer 22 ionospheric beacon satellite and photographically records its reflection.

4 February: Air Defense Command fighter pilots score their first interception of a Bomarc drone target. It was flying at more than 1,500 mph at an altitude of more than 50,000 feet.

8 February: The USAF performs its first retaliatory air strike in North Vietnam. A North American F–100 Super Sabre flies cover for attacking South Vietnamese fighter aircraft, suppressing ground fire in the target area.

18 February: First USAF jet raids are flown against enemy concentrations in South Vietnam. American pilots fly Martin B–57 Canberra bombers and F–100 fighters against the Vietcong in South Vietnam near An Khe.

1 March: As a test, the first launch of an ICBM from an operational base is made from Ellsworth AFB, South Dakota. A short-range, tethered, and unarmed Minuteman I missile is used.

5 March: USAF's F–111 completes its first supersonic flight at Fort Worth, Texas.

23 March: Gemini 3, the first two-man U.S. space capsule, is launched into orbit from the Air Force Eastern Test Range, Patrick AFB, Florida.

20 April: The last Atlas F to leave a SAC operational base is shipped from the 551st SMS, Lincoln AFB, Nebraska, to storage facilities for future use as a launch vehicle in various research and development programs. This completes the phaseout of SAC's first generation of ICBMs.

23 April: The first operational Lockheed C–141 Starlifter aircraft is delivered to Travis AFB, California.

2 May: An Oklahoma Air National Guard (ANG) "Talking Bird" C–97 command post flies to the Caribbean area to support U.S. forces in the Dominican Republic. Air Reserve transports airlift 4,547 tons of cargo and 5,436 passengers supporting the U.S. Air Force mission.

10 May: Tactical control of aircraft in battle areas is assigned to USAF by the Joint Chiefs of Staff.

4 June: USAF space pilots Majs James A. McDivitt and Edward H. White set a U.S. space endurance record lasting 97 hours, 30 seconds in a 63-orbit trip. During the Gemini 4 mission, White takes a 23-minute walk in space to become the first U.S. astronaut to accomplish this feat.

18 June: SAC B–52s are used for the first time in Vietnam when 28 aircraft, flying from Guam, strike Vietcong targets near Saigon.

29 June: X–15 hypersonic pilot Capt Joe Engle becomes the 12th and youngest pilot to receive astronaut wings.

30 June: The last of 800 Minuteman I ICBMs become operational at Francis E. Warren AFB when SAC accepts the fifth Minuteman wing from the AFSC.

10 July: Scoring the first U.S. Air Force air-to-air combat victory in Southeast Asia, two F–4C aircrews of the 45th

This picture of a painting from the USAF Art Collection, entitled "Victory Over North Vietnam," depicts a MiG–21 in flames after engaging a USAF F–4C.

Tactical Fighter Squadron down two communist MiG–17 jet fighters over North Vietnam.

7 August: The first Minuteman II missile is emplaced in its silo at Grand Forks AFB, North Dakota.

21 August: The Gemini 5 spacecraft carrying astronauts Lt Col Gordon Cooper, USAF, and Lt Cmdr Charles Conrad, USN, is launched into orbit by a Titan II booster. Splashdown will occur 29 August with a record-breaking 120 revolutions around the earth. It establishes five world records, including four previously held by the USSR.

14 October: The XB–70A Valkyrie flies at triple-sonic speed for the first time. The six-engine jet hits 2,000 mph at a 70,000-foot altitude.

15 October: The U.S. Air Force graduates the first class of 16 missile combat crew members from its Minuteman education program. SAC missilemen receive their master's degrees under a program sponsored by the Air University's Air Force Institute of Technology.

18 October: New York ANG's 107th Tactical Fighter Group becomes the first tactical guard unit deployed in peacetime to the Pacific for a joint-service exercise.

23 October: The 4503d Tactical Fighter Squadron (Provisional) arrives in Vietnam with 12 F–5A Freedom Fighter aircraft for combat evaluation tests. A fighter version of the T–38 Talon, the Freedom Fighter is produced for export.

31 October: The first ten Minuteman II missiles are transferred to SAC and are assigned to 447th Strategic Missile Squadron at Grand Forks AFB.

1 November: Col Jeanne M. Holm becomes director of WAF.

3 December: The Secretary of Defense announces the U.S. Air Force will develop a reconnaissance version of the F–111 Aardvark.

7 December: An operationally configured Minuteman II is fired by a SAC crew for the first time from an operational silo. The missile's reentry vehicle impacts approximately

4,000 miles downrange from the point of launch at Vandenberg AFB.

8 December: The Secretary of Defense announces plans to phase out older models of the B–52 bombers and all B–58 bombers.

10 December: Secretary McNamara announces the development of a strategic and tactical bomber version of the F–111, which will be known as the FB–111.

18 December: The 14-day flight by astronauts Cmdr James Lovell Jr. and Lt Col Frank Borman aboard the Gemini 7 spacecraft and the rendezvous with astronauts Lt Col Thomas P. Stafford and Capt Walter M. Schirra Jr., USN, in Gemini 6, complete the nation's most successful space mission. Gemini 7 establishes 11 world records for manned space flights, including the first rendezvous of two-manned maneuverable spacecraft and the longest manned space flight.

1966

1 January: The MATS is redesignated the Military Airlift Command (MAC). The Eastern and Western Air Transport Forces are redesignated the Twenty-first and Twenty-second Air Forces, respectively. The Air Rescue Service becomes the Aerospace Rescue and Recovery Service (ARRS). The Air Photographic and Charting Service is renamed the Aerospace Audio-Visual Service (AAVS).

1 January: Military airlift units of the ANG begin flying about 75 cargo flights a month to Southeast Asia. These flights are in addition to the more than 100 overseas missions flown in a month by the ANG in augmenting MAC's global airlift mission.

1 January: A large rocket facility is established at the Arnold Engineering Development Center, Tullahoma, Tennessee, to operate two high-altitude test cells.

22 January: Operation Blue Light, the largest airlift in history of troops and equipment into a combat zone, is completed. More than 4,600 tons of equipment and over

3,000 troops of the U.S. Army's 3d Infantry Brigade, are airlifted from Hickam AFB, Hawaii, to Pleiku, South Vietnam. The operation began 27 December 1965.

1 February: A 200-bed USAF hospital becomes operational at Cam Ranh Bay, South Vietnam.

16 February: Col L. Gordon Cooper, Col Frank Borman, and Lt Col Thomas P. Stafford receive astronaut wings from the U.S. Air Force Chief of Staff Gen John P. McConnell.

24 February: The first Minuteman salvo launch is made from Vandenberg AFB by a SAC missile combat crew from the 341st Strategic Missile Wing, Malmstrom AFB.

10 March: USAF Maj Bernard F. Fisher of Kuna, Idaho, a 1st Air Commando Squadron A–1E pilot, lands on the A Shau airstrip after it is overrun by North Vietnamese regulars to rescue downed A–1E pilot Maj Dafford W. Myers of Newport, Washington. Major Fisher is later awarded the Medal of Honor for his heroic act.

16 March: Titan II launches Neil Armstrong and David Scott on their Gemini 8 mission. The astronauts later accomplish the first docking maneuver in space with a Space Systems Division-developed Agena target vehicle launched by an Atlas booster. USAF pararescuemen attach flotation gear to the Gemini 8 space capsule 20 minutes after splashdown in the Pacific Ocean, 500 miles east of Okinawa. It is the first time USAF rescue forces have participated in the actual recovery of a Gemini capsule.

28 March: The USAF Special Weapons Center achieves the first successful midair catch of an air-launched, air-recoverable rocket (ALARR) nose cone over White Sands Missile Range.

31 March: SAC phases out its last B–47 Stratojet. The first all-jet strategic bomber entered active service in 1951.

5 April: The first successful voice communications test with airplane, satellite, and ground equipment is conducted in an Air Force Avionics Laboratory project.

6 April: The Army agrees to transfer its CV–2 Caribou and CV–7 Buffalo aircraft to the U.S. Air Force, which will be responsible for all future intratheater, fixed-wing tactical aircraft. USAF designations will be the C–7A Caribou and C–8A Buffalo.

12 April: SAC B–52 bombers strike targets in North Vietnam for the first time. They hit a supply route in the Mu Gia Pass about 85 miles north of the border.

25 April: SAC's first Minuteman II squadron—the 447th Strategic Missile Squadron, Grand Forks AFB—is declared combat ready. The squadron of 50 missiles and five launch-control facilities is transferred to SAC by the AFSC's Ballistic Systems Division.

26 April: Maj Paul J. Gilmore and 1st Lt William T. Smith become the first USAF pilots to destroy a MiG–21. Flying escort for F–105 Thunderchiefs near Hanoi when the flight is attacked, the F–4C pilots down the MiG with a Sidewinder missile.

5 May: USAF A–1E Skyraider pilots fly their first strikes against targets in North Vietnam.

3 June: NASA's Gemini 9 spacecraft with astronauts Lt Col Thomas P. Stafford, USAF, as command pilot and Lt Cmdr Eugene Cernan, USN, as pilot is successfully launched from the Eastern Test Range, Patrick AFB, by a Titan II booster. Personnel from various USAF commands provide support for the flight. Reentry is on 6 June.

16 June: USAF's Titan IIIC boosts seven experimental communications satellites and one gravity gradient satellite into orbit 18,000 nautical miles above the equator. The satellites demonstrate the feasibility of a global military communications satellite system.

1 July: The U.S. Air Force begins aeromedical evacuation flights from Saigon to the United States via Japan, reducing en route time to 24 hours.

9 July: The F–111 Aardvark variable-sweep-wing fighter-bomber flies for the first time at Mach 2.5—about 1,800 mph. Officials call the performance the highlight in the F–111 flight-test development program.

18 July: Gemini 10 is launched from the Air Force Eastern Test Range by a Titan booster with astronauts Cmdr John

Young, USN, as command pilot and Maj Michael Collins, USAF, as pilot. The astronauts soar to a new record altitude of more than 470 miles during the mission.

6 August: The nation's first three civilian scientist-astronauts—Owen K. Garriott, Edward G. Gibson, and Harrison H. Schmitt—receive USAF pilot wings at Williams AFB, Arizona.

25 August: The first class of German air force student pilots enters training at Sheppard AFB, Texas. The school will provide 212 pilots per year with training similar to that received by U.S. Air Force pilots.

20 September: Lt Col Donald M. Sorlie becomes the first USAF pilot to fly the NASA lifting body from the Air Force Flight Test Center. Air launched from a B–52 at an altitude of 45,000 feet, the craft reaches a speed of nearly 400 mph during the three and one-half-minute flight.

5 October: USAF begins operating a space-age communications system developed by the Electronic Systems Division. Spanning the Mediterranean from Spain to the Near East, the system provides rapid communications between commanders in that area and the United States. It is also used by the Army and Navy.

7 October: USAF selects the University of Colorado to conduct independent investigations into unidentified flying object (UFO) reports.

31 October: USAF announces its selection of the Boeing Company to develop and produce an air-to-surface short-range missile known as Maverick. Designated AGM–65A, the television-guided missile will be carried by the FB–111 and late model B–52 bombers.

9 November: USAF's F–111A fighter-bomber scores a first for American aircraft by flying faster than the speed of sound for 15 minutes at a constant ground clearance of less than 1,000 feet.

14 November: A MAC C–141 Starlifter is the first jet aircraft to land in the Antarctic. Commanded by Capt Howard Geddes, 86th Military Airlift Squadron, Travis AFB, the aircraft lands on the ice at McMurdo Sound after a 2,200-mile flight from Christchurch, New Zealand.

15 November: Tuy Hoa AB, the first air base in South Vietnam designed and constructed under U.S. Air Force supervision, becomes operational 45 days ahead of schedule. Actual construction of the base, known as Operation Turnkey, started in August 1966.

14 December: Col Albert R. Howarth demonstrates exemplary courage and airmanship under the most hazardous conditions of darkness and intense enemy fire while participating in a combat strike mission in Southeast Asia. Colonel Howarth wins the Mackay Trophy for this flight.

CHRONOLOGY

1967—1976

1967

2 January: F–4 Phantom pilots of the 8th Tactical Fighter Wing down seven MiG–21s over the Red River Valley, North Vietnam, to establish a one-day aerial victory record.

18 January: A Titan IIIC booster launched from Cape Kennedy sends eight military communications satellites into a near-perfect circular orbit.

27 January: Three of America's *Apollo* astronauts, USAF Lt Cols Virgil Grissom and Edward H. White and USN Lt Cmdr Robert B. Chaffee, are trapped and killed in a capsule by a flash fire while conducting a preflight rehearsal at Cape Kennedy.

6 February: The North American Aerospace Defense Command's Space Defense Center moves into Cheyenne Mountain, Colorado, completing the movement of all units into the hardened, underground facility.

Cargo awaits onload into a C–130 at an airstrip in South Vietnam. In the foreground are fuel bladders that have been emptied of JP–4 for use in Army helicopters.

22 February: Twenty-three USAF C–130s provide airlift for the first parachute personnel drop of the Vietnam War. The jump is made by the 173d Airborne Brigade in support of Operation Junction City.

24 February: Near Di Linh, South Vietnam, Capt Hilliard A. Wilbanks attacks a large body of Vietcong, who had ambushed a numerically inferior force of South Vietnamese rangers. Flying his unarmed and unarmored aircraft repeatedly over the enemy force, Captain Wilbanks uses smoke rockets and a rifle to draw the fire of the enemy and interrupt their advance. Mortally wounded on his last pass over the Vietcong, Captain Wilbanks sacrifices his life to protect the withdrawing rangers, earning the Medal of Honor for his bravery.

10 March: USAF F–105 Thunderchiefs and F–4C Phantom IIs bomb the Thai Nguyen steel plant in North Vietnam for the first time. During this attack, Capt Merlyn Hans Dethlefsen earns the Medal of Honor while silencing enemy defenses with his severely damaged F–105 Thunderchief despite intense enemy fire and fighter attacks.

10 March: Capt Mac C. Brestel, an F–105 Thunderchief pilot with the 355th Tactical Fighter Squadron, Takhli Royal Thai AFB, Thailand, becomes the first U.S. Air Force combat crewman to down two MiGs during a single mission.

15 March: The Sikorsky HH–53B, the largest and fastest helicopter in USAF inventory, makes its first flight. It is slated for ARRS operations in Southeast Asia.

21 March: Twelve SAC air crewmen are decorated by President Johnson at Andersen AFB, Guam, for B–52 bomber and KC–135 refueling missions to Vietnam.

30 March: A two-man submarine, the first USAF-owned underwater vessel, is added to AFSC's Western Test Range inventory. It will be used to locate reentry vehicles in the Eniwetok Atoll area.

3 April: Paul W. Airey becomes the first chief master sergeant of the U.S. Air Force.

8 April: Clove Hitch III, a joint exercise conducted in Puerto Rico under the Atlantic Command, opens with over 21,000 U.S. Army, Navy, Air Force, and National Guard personnel participating. This is the first time C–141s will be used to air-drop paratroopers.

9 April: The 315th Air Division begins the largest tactical unit move of the Vietnam War. Hercules C–130s airlift the entire 196th Light Infantry Brigade, including 3,500 troops and 4,000 tons of equipment, from Tay Ninh to Chu Lai during the five-day operation.

19 April: Maj Leo K. Thorsness earns the Medal of Honor for protecting the rescue of downed airmen in North Vietnamese territory. Flying an F–105 Thunderchief critically low on fuel, Major Thorsness shoots down one MiG–17, damages another, and drives off three more. Despite his urgent need for fuel, Major Thorsness elects to recover at a forward operating base, allowing another aircraft in emergency condition to refuel from an aerial tanker.

25 April: Maj Gen Benjamin D. Foulois, USAF, Retired, America's oldest military pilot, dies at Andrews AFB, Maryland.

28 April: A USAF Titan IIIC booster successfully orbits five unmanned satellites. They include two Vela nuclear-detection satellites and three scientific satellites.

29 April: The 1966 Daedalian Flight Safety Trophy, the nation's outstanding air safety award, is presented to MAC for a record fifth time.

30 April: The ALARR system has its first operational test. It is designed to detect and identify nuclear tests in the atmosphere.

13 May: For the second time pilots of the 8th Tactical Fighter Wing, Ubon Royal Thai AB, Thailand, shoot down seven MiGs in a single day's action over North Vietnam.

31 May: While piloting a KC–135 Stratotanker over the Gulf of Tonkin, Maj John H. Casteel and his three-man crew from the 902d Air Refueling Squadron accomplish a spectacular series of emergency refueling that saves six fuel-starved Navy fighters. The action earns Major Casteel and his crew the Mackay Trophy.

1 June: The Vietnamese air force officially accepts 20 F–5 aircraft, its first jets.

1 June: USAF crews fly two HH–3E helicopters nonstop from New York to Paris in 30 hours, 46 minutes, ten seconds with nine air refuelings.

9 June: The first O–2A Skymaster forward-air-controller aircraft arrives in Vietnam.

9 June: USAF begins the evacuation of about 1,300 military and civilian Americans to the United States from the Middle East because of Arab-Israeli war.

1 July: Civil Air Patrol national headquarters completes its move from Ellington AFB, Texas, to Maxwell AFB, Alabama.

1 July: A Titan IIIC booster launches six satellites into a circular, near-synchronous orbit. Included are three communications satellites, a scientific capsule, a gravity-measuring device, and an antenna test satellite.

11 July: First public rollout of the X–24A—a manned, flatiron-shaped wingless lifting body powered by a rocket engine to be used in atmospheric reentry studies.

13 July: Eighteen astronauts—nine from the Air Force, eight from the Navy, and one from the Marine Corps— receive the Distinguished Flying Cross for their Mercury and Gemini space flights.

13 August: The Alaskan Air Command, assisted by the Alaska ANG and other USAF units, begins a three-day rescue and support operation during a flood disaster in the Fairbanks area. Alaska-stationed Air Force Communications Service personnel provide emergency communications, and MAC provides airlift.

26 August: The North Vietnamese capture Maj George E. Day, a downed F-100 Super Sabre pilot who is severely wounded, and take him to a prison camp where he is interrogated and tortured. Despite his wounds, Major Day escapes and evades to the demilitarized zone where, delirious, he wanders aimlessly for several days until recaptured. Returned to the prison camp, the totally debilitated pilot continues to offer maximum resistance until his release in 1973. For his bravery, he receives the Medal of Honor.

9 September: Sgt Duane D. Hackney is presented the Air Force Cross for bravery during the rescue of an Air Force pilot in Vietnam. He is the first living enlisted man to receive the award.

3 October: Maj William J. Knight pilots the X–15 hypersonic rocket aircraft to a record 4,534 mph.

16 October: The first operational F–111A Aardvark supersonic tactical fighter lands at Nellis AFB, Nevada. It uses its terrain-following radar-guidance controls for the flight from Fort Worth, Texas.

24 October: U.S. planes attack North Vietnam's largest air base, Phuc Yen, for the first time in a combined Air Force, Navy, and Marine Corps strike. During the attack, the Air Force downs its 69th MiG.

9 November: Enemy gunners shoot down a helicopter piloted by Capt Gerald O. Young during USAF efforts to rescue an Army reconnaissance team near Khe Sanh, Republic of Vietnam. Captain Young survives the crash, and although badly burned, he aids another wounded crewman. Later, he attempts to divert hostile forces from the crash site. Refusing rescue because of the proximity of enemy forces, he successfully evades capture for 17 hours before finally being evacuated. Captain Young's bravery earns the Medal of Honor.

9 November–January: Capt Lance P. Sijan ejects from his F–4C Phantom over North Vietnam and successfully evades capture for more than six weeks. The enemy eventually captures him, but the severely weakened pilot manages to escape. Recaptured and tortured, he contracts pneumonia and dies. Captain Sijan received the Medal of Honor posthumously.

15 November: Maj Michael J. Adams is killed in an X–15 hypersonic crash, the first fatality since the program began in 1959.

17 November: Operation Eagle Thrust, the largest and greatest distance airlift of troops and cargo from the U.S. to Southeast Asia, begins by C-141 Starlifters and C-130 Hercules aircraft. During the operation, 10,356 paratroopers and 5,118 tons of equipment are airlifted to the combat zone in record time.

1968

1 January: The Reserve Forces Bill of Rights and Vitalization Act becomes law. The Office of Air Force Reserve is established as part of the Air Staff to serve as a policy planning center for Reserve operations.

5 January: The Air Force Academy implements the T-41 Mescalero Light Plane Flying Program.

12 January: USAF announces a system by which tactical air units will carry with them all they need to operate at "bare" bases equipped only with runways, taxiways, parking areas, and a water supply.

16 January: United States Air Forces Europe (USAFE) and MAC crews provide a six-day airlift of food and equipment to Sicilian earthquake victims.

21 January: Communists begin a 77-day siege of the U.S. Marine Corps stronghold at Khe Sanh, South Vietnam, which results in a victory for U.S. air power over enemy ground forces.

26 January: ANG and Air Force Reserve (AFRES) elements are called to active duty because of the USS *Pueblo* incident and increased enemy activity in Vietnam.

3 February: At AFSC's Arnold Engineering Development Center, Tullahoma, a laser beam is used for the first time as a light source for photographing aircraft and missile models at high velocity.

14 February: Continental Air Command's AFRES military airlift units assist MAC in routine missions, while MAC participates in the rapid deployment of elements of the 82d Airborne Division and over 3,000 marines and equipment to Southeast Asia.

28 February: The last of 284 C–141 Starlifter cargo aircraft purchased by USAF is delivered to Tinker AFB, Oklahoma.

29 February: Aircraft attached to USAF's Southern Command deliver emergency supplies to flood-stricken Bolivia.

29 February: Col Jeanne M. Holm, WAF director, and Col Helen O'Day, assigned to the Office of the Air Force Chief of Staff, become the first USAF women promoted to the permanent rank of colonel under the public law that removed the restriction of the promotion of women to higher ranks in all the armed services.

19 March: The first class of 12 South Vietnamese air force pilots begin A–37 Dragonfly training at England AFB, Louisiana.

25 March: F–111 Aardvarks fly their first combat mission in Southeast Asia against military targets in North Vietnam.

25 March: The 944th Military Airlift Group (Associate) is activated at Norton AFB, California, becoming the first Air Force Reserve Group to function under the new associate unit concept. The Reserve associate unit's personnel fly and maintain aircraft assigned to the associated active force unit.

31 March: President Johnson directs a halt in U.S. bombing north of the 20th parallel in North Vietnam.

28 April: USAF's Southern Command C–130 Hercules crews airlift approximately 92,000 pounds of food to La Toma, Ecuador, a drought-stricken area, over a 13-day period.

1 May: ANG tactical refueling units complete one year of overseas duty on a continuous basis without mobilization. This is the first operation of its type in Guard/Reserve history.

3 May: The first ANG unit called to active duty in the Vietnam conflict, the 120th Tactical Fighter Squadron, arrives in South Vietnam and begins flying combat missions two days later.

12 May: Lt Col Joe M. Jackson lands his C–123 Provider aircraft on a special forces camp airstrip that is being overrun by hostile forces. Despite intense enemy fire including light artillery, Colonel Jackson rescues a three-man combat control team, earning the Medal of Honor for his bravery.

16 May: USAF airlifts 88.5 tons of food and relief material to Ethiopia in response to a flood emergency.

13 June: A Titan IIIC launch vehicle successfully places in orbit eight communications satellites from Cape Kennedy augmenting the initial defense satellite communications system.

17 June: The first C–9 Nightingale aeromedical evacuation aircraft ordered by MAC for airlift of patients within the United States is rolled out at McDonnell-Douglas Corporation, Long Beach, California.

19 June: A "fast-fix" cement that hardens in only 30 minutes is developed for helicopter landing sites by AFSC's Aero Propulsion Laboratory, Wright-Patterson AFB, Ohio, and is tested in Southeast Asia.

30 June: The Lockheed C–5 Galaxy, USAF's newest and largest aircraft, makes its first flight.

31 July: Two UH–1F helicopters from USAF's Southern Command help the Costa Rican government evacuate people endangered by the eruption of Mount Arenal.

1 August: Continental Air Command is discontinued and Headquarters AFRES is established at Robins AFB, Georgia. The Air Reserve Personnel Center at Denver, Colorado, is established as a separate operating agency.

1 August: USAF's Southern Command flies 13,000 pounds of disaster relief supplies to San Jose, Costa Rica, to aid the victims in the Mount Arenal volcano eruption.

16 August: The first Minuteman III missile is successfully launched from Cape Kennedy. Equipped with multiple independently targetable reentry vehicles, the Minuteman III ICBM can attack three targets simultaneously.

21 August: An estimated 260 people are evacuated and 52,000 pounds of food and personal belongings are airlifted by a USAF UH–1F helicopter during a four-day period aiding flood victims in northeastern Nicaragua.

25 August: The North American OV–10 Bronco, the U.S. Air Force's newest forward air controller aircraft, begins a 90-day combat evaluation program in South Vietnam.

1 September: While an on-scene commander in the attempted rescue of a downed American pilot, Lt Col William A. Jones III repeatedly flies his A1–H Skyraider aircraft over enemy gun emplacements, sustaining heavy aircraft damage and severe burns. Discovering his radio transmitters are inoperative, Colonel Jones refuses to egress his crippled aircraft and, in extreme pain, flies back to base where he reports the downed pilot's location. Colonel Jones receives the Medal of Honor for his gallantry.

11 October: USAF units support the first manned space mission in NASA's Apollo project when three astronauts, among them USAF Maj Donn F. Eisele, are launched in the *Apollo 7* capsule into an 11-day earth orbit from Cape Kennedy.

1 November: President Johnson halts all bombing of North Vietnam.

26 November: Piloting a UH–1F helicopter, 1st Lt James P. Fleming twice exposes his aircraft to intense hostile fire while attempting to rescue a special forces reconnaissance patrol. Finally rescuing the patrol, Lieutenant Fleming returns to base, eventually receiving the Medal of Honor for his gallantry.

21 December: NASA's *Apollo 8* begins a seven-day mission from Cape Kennedy with various USAF units supporting the mission. The astronauts USAF Cols Frank Borman and William A. Anders and USN Capt James A. Lovell Jr. achieve man's first circumlunar space travel.

1969

1 January: The first AC–119 Shadow gunship combat mission in Vietnam is flown by the AFRES 71st Special Operations Squadron.

4 February: The XB–70 Valkyrie research aircraft is flown to Wright-Patterson AFB, Ohio, to become part of the Air Force Museum's exhibit of outstanding and historic aircraft.

9 February: The free world's first tactical communications satellite, the 1,600-pound TACSAT 1, is boosted into a geostationary orbit from the Air Force Eastern Test Range, Florida, by a Titan IIIC launch vehicle. TACSAT satellites are designed to relay communications among small land-mobile, airborne, or shipborne tactical stations.

24 February: During a night mission in support of a South Vietnamese army post, an AC–47 gunship on which A1C John L. Levitow serves as loadmaster is struck by an enemy mortar shell. Although seriously wounded and stunned, Airman Levitow flings himself on a smoking magnesium flare rolling in the cargo compartment, drags it to an open cargo door, and ejects it. Almost immediately the flare ignites clear of the aircraft. For this selfless heroism, Levitow becomes the fourth enlisted airman to win the Medal of Honor and the only enlisted airman to win the nation's highest military honor in Vietnam.

3–13 March: The *Apollo 9* crew, consisting of USAF Cols James A. McDivitt and David R. Scott and civilian Russell L. Schweikart, begins testing the lunar module while in the earth's orbit. The crew also makes the first transfer between space vehicles using an internal connection.

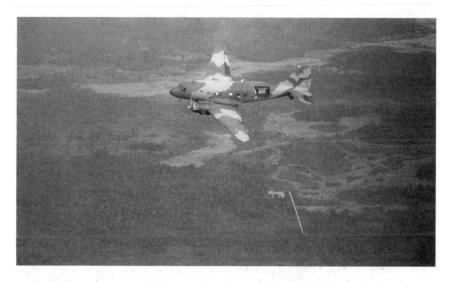

An AC–47 Dragonship fires its miniguns at a target on the ground. The streak is from tracer bullets just fired from the aircraft's guns.

18 March: Three satellites containing 17 experiments in the Orbiting Vehicle Program are launched from Vandenberg AFB under the direction of the Office of Aerospace Research scientists to conduct basic environmental research in near-earth orbits.

4–10 April: The 49th Tactical Fighter Wing redeploys its 72 F–4D aircraft from Spangdahlem AB, Germany, to Holloman AFB, New Mexico, accomplishing 504 successful aerial refuelings. The wing receives the Mackay Trophy for the redeployment.

11 April: The first Minuteman III ICBM launch at Vandenberg AFB is accomplished by a SAC combat missile crew under the direction of technicians from the AFSC.

17 April: The first free flight of the X–24 lifting body is completed at the Air Force Flight Test Center, Edwards AFB, with Maj Jerauld R. Gentry at the controls.

14 May: USAF's Southern Command personnel begin a massive U.S. Air Force/State Department/Public Health Service campaign to combat an encephalitis epidemic in Ecuador.

18–26 May: Climaxing the *Apollo 10* mission, astronauts Col Thomas Stafford, USAF, and Cmdr Eugene A. Cernan, USN, approach within nine miles of the lunar surface in the lunar module *Snoopy*.

4 June: The Thunderbirds, the USAF Air Demonstration Squadron, hold their first exhibition using the F–4 Phantom aircraft.

10 June: AFSC presents the number one X–15 hypersonic rocket-powered, manned research aircraft to the Smithsonian Institution, Washington, D. C., for display with other historic aircraft.

1 July: USAF service numbers are replaced by social security account numbers for all military personnel.

8 July: The first of 25,000 troops withdrawn from Southeast Asia under the administration's Vietnamization policy are airlifted aboard C–141 Starlifters from Vietnam to McChord AFB, Washington.

16 July: The launch of *Apollo 11*, the first manned lunar landing mission, is supported by USAF personnel world-wide.

17 July: Alaskan Air Command assumes responsibility for resupplying T–3 (Fletcher's Ice Island) with food, fuel, equipment, and supplies. T–3 is a floating, 20-square-mile island used for weather and other scientific research.

19 July: USAF's Southern Command personnel and aircraft airlift emergency supplies as part of its role in a seven-nation team helping to mediate a cease-fire in the Honduras–El Salvador conflict.

Apollo 11 astronaut Edwin E. "Buzz" Aldrin Jr., an Air Force colonel, walks on the surface of the moon. Fellow astronaut Neil Armstrong took this photo with the lunar surface camera.

20 July: The *Apollo 11* mission reaches the moon. The first man on the moon is Neil Armstrong, a civilian. USAF Col Edwin E. Aldrin Jr. becomes the second man to set foot on the moon. While the two astronauts spend nearly three hours exploring the surface, Lt Col Michael Collins, USAF, orbits the moon in the command module for 59 hours, 27 minutes, 55 seconds. The *Apollo 11* crew will later receive numerous awards, including, in 1970, the Gen Thomas D. White Space Trophy, the Collier Trophy, and the Harmon Trophy.

25 August: MAC crews complete the first aerial refueling of the C–5 Galaxy jet cargo transport.

2 September: Scientists at the Air Force Cambridge Research Laboratory's Lunar Laser Observatory bounce a laser signal off the retroreflector placed on the moon by *Apollo 11* astronauts.

8 October: Helicopter crews from the 58th Aerospace Rescue and Recovery Squadron, Wheelus AB, Libya, save the lives of more than 2,500 Tunisians during a six-day rescue mission and airlift food, water, clothing, and medicine to the flood-stricken area.

29 October: SAC announces the phaseout of all B–58 Hustler strategic bombers from USAF inventory. The Hustler entered operational service in August 1960.

14 November: USAF personnel at locations throughout the world support the *Apollo 12* launch and recovery operations.

17 December: USAF concludes the UFO reporting and investigating project designated "Blue Book."

18 December: Air Force Missile Development Center crews complete the first guided launch of the Maverick (AGM–65) missile—an air-to-surface television-guided missile capable of attacking close-in targets in movement.

23 December: McDonnell Douglas is named prime contractor for the USAF's F–15 Eagle air-superiority fighter. With a top speed of 920 mph, the heavily armed fighter will have a ferry range of 3,450 nautical miles.

1970

5 January: Aerospace Defense Command's Backup Intercept Control (BUIC) III radar system becomes fully operational with the acceptance of the facility at the 80th Air Defense Group, Fortuna AFS, North Dakota. Designed to provide immediate information on any airborne threat to the North American continent, the BUIC III system augments the SAGE system.

10 January: AFSC engineers at Kirtland AFB, New Mexico, test a small, portable water treatment plant capable of producing 4,000 gallons of drinking water a day from sewage.

17 January: Reserve aircrews airlift carpenters and painters to New Orleans, Louisiana, to help repair damage caused by Hurricane Camille.

27 January: The first increment of a 64-man Air Training Command mobile training team is deployed to Vietnam to assist in the establishment of 17 basic maintenance training courses. These courses form the foundation of training to support further expansion of the Vietnamese air force capabilities.

30 January: Operational control of the first Skynet communications satellite is turned over to the United Kingdom after launch and orbit insertion on 8 January by AFSC's Space and Missile Systems Organization.

3 February: USAF rescue crews from the 36th Aerospace Rescue and Recovery Squadron, Yokota AB, begin rescue of 44 seamen from one ship sinking and 59 seamen involved in another ship sinking in the North Pacific—the Liberian freighter *Antonious Demades* and the Japanese freighter *California Maru.*

27 February: The first F–111E arrives at the Air Force Flight Test Center, Edwards AFB, for flight testing.

27 February: DOD selects Pratt and Whitney Aircraft to develop and produce engines for USAF F–15 and Navy F–14B aircraft.

15 March: The overseas portion of the worldwide automatic voice network (AUTOVON) is completed, making it possible to call any U.S. military installation in the world.

19 March: The X–24 lifting body successfully completes its first powered flight over Edwards AFB. It is piloted by Maj Jerauld R. Gentry, a test pilot at the Air Force Flight Test Center.

20 March: The first of two communications satellites for the North Atlantic Treaty Organization is launched from the Air Force Eastern Test Range, Cape Kennedy AFS, on a Thor-Delta booster.

24 March: The President mobilizes certain AFRES and ANG units to support the U.S. Post Office during a strike by postal employees.

24 March: The first launching of the Bomarc "B" guided missile, using the new BUIC III computerized command and control equipment, is completed at Tyndall AFB, Florida.

30 March: USAFE dispatches medical teams and support personnel from units in Turkey to provide medical aid and other humanitarian services to thousands of earthquake victims of Gediz, Turkey, and surrounding villages.

31 March: Phaseout of the last Mace missile is completed. The missiles are stored at the Military Aircraft Storage and Disposition Center, Davis-Monthan AFB, for possible use as subsonic target drones.

1 April: SAC's postattack command and control system is reorganized and relocated to inland operating bases at Offutt AFB, Nebraska; Grissom AFB, Indiana; and Ellsworth AFB, North Dakota.

10 April: Air Training Command completes shipment of 872 trainers under Project Pacer Bravo in support of the Vietnamese air force improvement and modernization program.

11 April: TAC gains its first ANG tactical airlift unit when the 146th Tactical Airlift Wing, California ANG, is formally reorganized.

11 April: Personnel and aircraft from the USAF's Southern Command begin an assistance program for flood victims in Costa Rica and Panama. Thirty-eight are dead and thousands left homeless.

11–17 April: The USAF supports launch and recovery of the disastrous *Apollo 13* flight, which was aborted 56 hours into the mission because of mechanical failures.

14 April: The first airlift of an operational Minuteman III missile is accomplished by a C–141 Starlifter. The missile is airlifted from Hill AFB, Utah, to Minot AFB, North Dakota.

4 May: A SAC task force of four B–52s wins the Blue Steel Trophy for best results in combined bombing and navigation during the Royal Air Force (RAF) Strike Command bombing and navigation competition at RAF Station, Marham, England.

5 May: Air Force Reserve Officer Training Corps expands to include women after test programs at Ohio State, Drake, East Carolina, and Auburn Universities prove successful.

8 May: An AC–119K Shadow gunship attacks one of the most heavily defended road sections in Southeast Asia. Despite the loss of 15 feet of the aircraft's right wing and one aileron, the crew destroys three enemy supply trucks and successfully returns to base. For this feat, the crew will receive the Mackay Trophy.

2 June: USAF's Southern Command personnel and aircraft from Howard and Albrook AFBs, Canal Zone, and C–130s from Lockbourne AFB, Ohio, begin massive disaster relief operations for victims of a devastating earthquake in Peru that killed 70,000 and left 800,000 homeless. In 31 days, USAFSO crews airlift 1.5 million pounds of supplies and equipment and 2,827 passengers and make 501 medical evacuations, while operating under practically bare-base conditions 1,500 miles from their home base.

5 June: North American Rockwell (airframe) and General Electric (engines) contracts are signed for engineering a development of the B–1, the proposed follow-on weapon system to replace the B–52 aircraft.

6 June: Gen Jack J. Catton, commander, MAC, accepts delivery of the first C-5 for operational use in the Air Force.

19 June: The first flight of Minuteman III missiles becomes operational at Minot AFB.

22 June: A USAF PRIME BEEF (Base Engineer Emergency Force) team from Chanute AFB, Illinois, restores the water system to Crescent City, Illinois, following explosions and fire that wiped out the business district.

5 July: The first contract for the new airborne warning and control system (AWACS) aircraft is let to the Boeing Company. The AWACS fleet serves as airborne combat direction centers for Aerospace Defense Command.

14 July: The C-5 Galaxy completes its first transpacific flight of 21,500 miles, inaugurating service to Hickam AFB; Andersen AFB; Clark AB, Republic of the Philippines; and Kadena AB, Okinawa.

20 July: Electronics Systems Division, L. G. Hanscom Field, Massachusetts, turns over to the Air Force Communications Service the recently completed photo relay system known as Compass Link. Using three ground stations and two satellites, Compass Link can transmit exposed film from Southeast Asia to the Pentagon via electronic signals and laser beams.

31 July: The first class of Vietnamese students under the president's Vietnamization Program completes the Undergraduate Pilot Training course at Keesler AFB, Mississippi.

August: Secretary of Defense Melvin Laird announces the Total Force Concept of the armed services. USAF incorporates capabilities of Air Force Reserve and Air National Guard (together, the Air Reserve Forces) into all aspects of planning and budgeting. These forces also take on a far greater role in normal USAF operations.

4 August: Aircrews of the AFRES airlift 73 mentally and physically handicapped children from Corpus Christi to Austin, Texas, after Hurricane Celia destroyed their school.

6 August: The United States and Spain sign a five-year agreement allowing the United States to continue shared use of four Spanish military bases. In return, the United States will contribute to the modernization of the Spanish armed forces.

24 August: Two USAF search and rescue helicopters, HH–53 Sea Stallions, successfully complete the first nonstop transpacific helicopter crossing in a 9,000-mile ferry flight from Eglin AFB to Da Nang Airport, Vietnam.

17 September–28 October: C–130 Hercules cargo aircraft assigned to the USAFE and MAC participate in Operation Fig Hill, transporting food, medical supplies, and equipment to Jordan. The supplies relieve suffering resulting from internal conflict.

2 October: The USAF Special Operations Force, Hurlburt Field, Florida, takes possession of the new UH–1N Bell Twin Huey. It is the first operational unit in the Air Force to have the helicopter.

11 October: The first USAF Undergraduate Helicopter Pilot Training student enters training at Fort Wolters, Texas. The U.S. Army trains 225 helicopter pilots for the Air Force annually.

21 October: The X–24A aerospace vehicle makes its first supersonic speed-flight at the Air Force Flight Test Center, Edwards AFB.

27 October: Doctors at Wilford Hall USAF Medical Center, Lackland AFB, develop a new device to save infants who are suffocating. Costing only about $1,000 and built from various standard hospital components, the device gives physicians precise control over pressure, composition, and volume of air, oxygen, and mists to help newborn babies breathe.

1 November: During their off-duty time, USAF physicians assigned to USAF Hospital, Wurtsmith AFB, Michigan, begin free medical care for nearby Chippewa native American residents under the Domestic Action Program.

1 November: The 336th Tactical Fighter Squadron begins testing new bare-base mobility equipment in a field exercise at North Field, South Carolina. The exercise demonstrates the capability to deploy to and operate from a bare-base site using specially designed air-transportable expendable shelters and work facilities, including dormitories, workshops, hangars, control towers, medical facilities, and electric and water systems.

13 November: An initial class of 100 USAF medical technicians begins specialized clinical training to qualify them to perform many of the tasks previously performed by doctors. Graduates will suture wounds, apply and remove casts and dressings, and accomplish routine physical examinations.

17 November: C–141 Starlifters of MAC begin the airlift of men and equipment to Dacca, East Pakistan, to aid that country's recovery from massive tidal waves.

20 November: USAF's Southern Command celebrates its 30th anniversary as a major air command, while its aircraft and personnel assist Colombians hard hit by floods.

21 November: A special task force of Air Force and Army volunteers make a daring but unsuccessful attempt to rescue American servicemen from the Son Tay prisoner-of-war (POW) camp 20 miles west of Hanoi. Brig Gen Leroy J. Manor leads the mission and is one of 39 USAF personnel participating in the effort.

5 December: Air Force Reservists from the 945th Military Airlift Group, Hill AFB, assist in a domestic action program to provide 40,000 pounds of food and clothing to Navajo native Americans on reservations spanning the corners of four states.

16 December: The 509th Bombardment Wing, Pease AFB, New Hampshire, receives the first FB–111A Aardvark assigned to a SAC combat unit.

1971

8 January: USAF's first tactical squadron of Minuteman III missiles is completed by AFSC at Minot AFB. The squadron consists of five manned launch-control centers and 50 unmanned silo launchers.

21–25 February: More than 1,200 national guardsmen assist in disaster relief operations in six states hit by tornadoes, snowstorms, and earthquakes. ANG participation includes the airdrop of 300 tons of hay to snowbound cattle by C–124 aircraft assigned to the Oklahoma ANG.

27 February: USAF launches Operation Haylift in response to urgent pleas from farmers in blizzard-swept Kansas and drops 35,000 bales (nearly a million pounds) of hay for 275,000 cattle stranded in deep snow. The hay is provided by the American Humane Society.

2 March: USAF introduces a policy permitting women who become pregnant to remain on active duty or to be discharged and return to duty within 12 months of discharge.

10 March: Ten Japanese fishermen shipwrecked 200 miles southwest of Kadena, Okinawa, are saved from rough surf and a coral reef by an Air Force helicopter crew.

17 March: Jane Leslie Holley becomes the first woman commissioned through the Air Force Reserve Officer Training Corps program. She graduated from Auburn University in Alabama.

18 March: Capt Marcelite C. Jordon becomes the first woman aircraft maintenance officer after completing the Aircraft Maintenance Officer School.

7 April: 2d Lt Susanne M. Ocobock becomes the first woman civil engineer in the Air Force and is assigned to Kelly AFB, Texas.

26 April: Crewing an SR–71 Blackbird strategic reconnaissance aircraft assigned to the 9th Strategic Reconnaissance Wing, Lt Col Thomas B. Estes, aircraft commander, and Maj Dewain C. Vick, reconnaissance systems officer, make a record-breaking 15,000-mile nonstop flight, at time attaining speeds in excess of Mach 3.

16 June–18 July: Four C–130s from Pope AFB, North Carolina, fly 308 sorties in Operation Bonny Jack, the humanitarian airlift of East Pakistani refugees from the Indian border state of Tripura to resettlement areas in Gauhati, further inland. On return flights they carry more than 1,750 tons of rice to feed refugees remaining in Tripura. On the initial deployment from the continental U.S., the C–130s deliver one million doses of anticholera vaccine to India.

1 July: Selfridge AFB, Michigan, is turned over by the Aerospace Defense Command to the ANG. It is the first major active USAF base to come under control of the Air Guard.

11–22 July: Seven UC–123K Providers from Langley AFB and Hurlburt Field and eight C–47 Skytrains from England AFB spray more than 2.5 million acres in southeastern Texas with malathion to combat an outbreak of Venezuelan Equine Encephalomyelitis. The operation, conducted in conjunction with the U.S. Department of Agriculture, is nicknamed Combat Vee.

16 July: Jeanne M. Holm, director of WAF, is promoted to brigadier general, becoming the first woman to attain general officer rank in the Air Force.

23 July: Hughes Aircraft Company is awarded a $70 million contract to build 2,000 Maverick (AGM–65A) air-to-surface missiles for use on F–4E and A–7D aircraft.

26 July: With an all-Air Force crew composed of Col David R. Scott, Lt Col James B. Irwin, and Maj Alfred M. Worden, *Apollo 15* blasts off from Cape Kennedy. The mission is described as the most scientifically important and, potentially, the most perilous lunar trip since the first landing. Millions of viewers throughout the world watch as color TV cameras cover Scott and Irwin as they explore the lunar surface using a moon-rover vehicle for the first time.

29 July: The experimental USAF X–24A lifting body completes its flight-test program.

10 September: The USAF's 17th Special Operations Squadron flies its final AG–119G gunship mission and begins transferring its aircraft to the Vietnamese air force. Nicknamed Shadow for its close air support and interdiction of enemy supply lines on night missions, the AC–119 aircraft are the first gunships assigned to the Vietnamese, who operate them from Tan Son Nhut AB.

12–16 September: Three USAF aircraft fly to Nicaragua to assist disaster relief operations in the aftermath of Hurricane Edith. Cargo includes food, medical supplies, tents, a USAF radio jeep to assist in the coordination of emergency operations, and fuel for rescue helicopters.

14 September: Fifteen USAF C–7 Caribou aircraft begin a ten-day, 8,000-mile return flight to McClellan AFB, California, from Cam Ranh Bay AB, Vietnam. While in Southeast Asia, the transport aircraft flew from unimproved airstrips providing fresh foodstuffs and supplies to otherwise inaccessible outposts.

1972

31 January: Air Training Command accepts its last T–38 Talon aircraft (tail no. 70-1956) at Palmdale, California.

17 February: Air Force One, a VC–137 Stratoliner aircraft belonging to the 89th Military Airlift Wing, departs Andrews AFB, Maryland, carrying President and Mrs. Nixon on their historic trip to China to meet with Chinese premier Chou En-Lai.

1 March: The first production line short-range attack missile is delivered to SAC.

April: In Operation Constant Guard, following the North Vietnamese spring offensive, MAC helps move the 49th Tactical Fighter Wing's 3,195 airmen and 1,600 tons of cargo from Holloman AFB to Takhli, Thailand, in nine days.

1 April: Air Training Command activates the Community College of the Air Force at Randolph AFB.

6 April: American aircraft and warships begin heavy, sustained attacks on North Vietnam for the first time since cessation of bombing in October 1968.

10 April: B–52 Stratofortress aircraft resume deep penetration raids that had been halted since 31 October 1968 into North Vietnam.

27 April: Four USAF fighter crews, releasing Paveway I laser-guided "smart" bombs, knock down the Thanh Hoa bridge in North Vietnam. Previously, 871 conventional

A B–52 unloads on ground targets in Vietnam.

sorties resulted in only superficial damage to the bridge. This raid introduces precision-guided munitions into combat for the first time.

May: The last B–57 Intruder aircraft leaves Southeast Asia and returns to the United States, ending its combat career.

12 May: A C–130 Hercules aircraft flies 5,000 pounds of civilian-donated medical equipment from Stuttgart, Germany, to a new hospital at Sile, Turkey.

26 May: President Nixon and Soviet General Secretary Leonid I. Brezhnev sign a Strategic Arms Limitation (SAL) agreement. This limits the number of land- and sea-based launchers for both sides.

11 June: B–52 Stratofortress aircraft using laser-guided bombs destroy a major hydroelectric plant near Hanoi, North Vietnam.

27 June: USAF C–123 Provider aircraft operations in Southeast Asia come to a halt with the transfer of the aircraft to the Vietnamese air force.

29 June: Forward air controller Capt Steven L. Bennett and his observer spot enemy troops attacking a friendly unit.

Denied tactical air and artillery support for the embattled unit, Captain Bennett strafes the enemy, forcing a retreat, but a surface-to-air missile hits the OV–10 Bronco, crippling it and shredding the observer's parachute. Captain Bennett, knowing that the observer cannot bail out, elects to ditch the OV–10 in the Gulf of Tonkin. He is killed in the crash landing, but his observer survives. For his heroic sacrifice, Captain Bennett posthumously receives the Medal of Honor.

11 July: USAF launches a giant 962-foot-tall balloon system in support of NASA's Viking Project for landing an unmanned spacecraft on Mars in 1976.

26 July–25 August: In response to flooding, Pacific Air Forces (PACAF) airlifts over four million pounds of food and medical supplies to the Philippine Islands.

27 July: The first flight of the F–15 Eagle advanced tactical fighter at Air Force Flight Test Center, Edwards AFB, is accomplished ahead of schedule.

11 August: The first flight of the F–5E international fighter aircraft is made at Edwards AFB, marking the beginning of contractor development, test, and evaluation.

19–20 August: The USAF HH–3 Jolly Green Giant and HH–43 Huskie helicopters save a total of 763 Korean civilians from rising waters when heavy rains cause the Han River, South Korea, to flood.

28 August: Capt Richard S. "Steve" Ritchie, flying with Capt Charles B. DeBellevue, his backseater, becomes the Vietnam War's first ace by shooting down his fifth MiG–21. Captain DeBellevue shoots down his fifth MiG two weeks later. For their achievements, the two aces will share the 1972 Mackay Trophy with Capt Jeffrey S. Feinstein, the third USAF ace of the Vietnam War.

11 September: Using precision-guided munitions, U.S. aircraft destroy the Long Bien bridge over the Red River in downtown Hanoi, North Vietnam.

15 September: The 42d Bombardment Wing, Loring AFB, Maine, becomes the first B–52 Stratofortress wing to be operational with the short-range attack missile.

13 October: Capt Jeffrey S. Feinstein achieves ace status by shooting down his fifth MiG–21.

23 October: Linebacker I B–52 operations against North Vietnam are halted when bombing north of the 20th parallel is curtailed.

31 October: The last Bomarc surface-to-air missile squadron, the 22d Air Defense Missile Squadron, Langley AFB, is inactivated.

22 November: The first B–52 Stratofortress aircraft lost to enemy action is hit by a surface-to-air missile while on a mission over North Vietnam. The aircraft crashes in Thailand, where the crew ejects and is recovered.

18 December: President Nixon directs the resumption of full-scale bombing and mining in North Vietnam, in an operation known as Linebacker II.

18–29 December: Supporting Linebacker II, KC–135 Stratotanker aircraft fly more than 1,300 sorties.

30 December: President Nixon orders a halt to the bombing of North Vietnam north of the 20th parallel and announces that peace talks will resume in Paris on 8 January 1973.

1973

8 January: An F–4D Phantom shoots down a MiG southwest of Hanoi with a radar-guided AIM–7 missile. This is the last aerial victory before the signing of the cease-fire that goes into effect on 29 January.

22 January: President Johnson dies. The *Spirit of 76*, a VC–137, flies his body from Texas to Washington, D.C. for a final tribute.

27 January: In Paris, North Vietnam and the United States sign an "Agreement on Ending the War and Restoring Peace to Vietnam."

28 January: A B–52 Stratofortress bombs targets in South Vietnam at 0628 hours local time. This sortie ends Arc Light operations, which have been continuous since 1965.

12 February: MAC pilots initiate Operation Homecoming, flying the first of 590 released American prisoners of war from Hanoi, North Vietnam, to Clark AB. The Mackay Trophy is awarded to the aircrews of MAC.

21 February: The 30-year civil war in Laos officially ends, and a cease-fire prevails. The United States halts air strikes.

21 March: Two Libyan Mirage aircraft intercept and fire upon an unarmed Rhein-Main-based (Germany) C–130 Hercules aircraft, reportedly on a reconnaissance mission over the Mediterranean. The C–130 successfully evades its attackers and lands safely at Athenai Airport, Greece.

28 March: The final flight of PACAF aircraft departs South Vietnam for redeployment on 28 March 1973.

13 April: USAFE accepts responsibility for manning and operating a program to train the Iranian air force in F–4 Phantom aircraft operations.

16 April: U.S. aircraft resume bombing North Vietnamese positions in Laos following reports that the Communists had overrun a town in the *Plaine des Jarres.*

18 May: Lockheed of Georgia delivers the 81st and last production model of the C–5A Galaxy aircraft to USAF.

15 July: An A–7D Corsair of the 354th Tactical Reconnaissance Wing flies the last combat mission of the Southeast Asian War. All told, USAF flew 5.25 million sorties over South Vietnam, North Vietnam, northern and southern Laos, and Cambodia, losing 2,251 aircraft—1,737 to hostile action and 514 for other operational reasons.

6 September: The 561st Tactical Fighter Squadron (F–105 Thunderchief aircraft) leaves Korat Royal Thai AB, Thailand, bound for George AFB, California.

30 September: Air Training Command inactivates Laredo AFB, Texas, and places it in caretaker status.

October: The Air Weather Service declares operational at Elmendorf AFB a ground-based liquid-propane system for dissipating cold fog. Using this system will allow more air traffic during inclement weather.

13 October–13 November: During the Yom Kippur War, American airlifters supporting Operation Nickel Grass fly 567 sorties from the United States, delivering 22,318 tons of war materiel to Israel. Regular and Reserve units participated.

20 October: As a consequence of the Arab-Israeli conflict, the Arab nations declare an oil embargo that disrupts flying training.

28 October: The first production model of the T–43 aircraft arrives at Mather AFB, California.

19 December: USAF approves procurement of 52 A–10 Thunderbolt production aircraft, associated engines, and the GAU–8A 30 mm gun system. This follows a successful flight evaluation fly-off of the A–10 with the A–7D Corsair.

1974

16–19 January: The 48th Air Rescue and Recovery Squadron evacuates 93 persons from flooded areas near Pinehurst, Idaho.

10 April: USAFE C–130 Hercules aircraft, crews, and communications personnel support Operation Nimbus Star, the mine-sweeping operation required to clear the Suez Canal of obstacles prior to navigation.

May: The 354th Tactical Fighter Wing completes its redeployment from Korat, Thailand, to Myrtle Beach, South Carolina.

5 July: The 555th Tactical Fighter Squadron moves without personnel or equipment from Udorn Royal Thai AB to Luke AFB to become the first F–15 Eagle squadron in the USAF.

29 July: Secretary of Defense James R. Schlesinger directs the U.S. Air Force to consolidate all military airlift aircraft under a single manager. USAF will be the single manager for all armed services.

4 August: The 8th Tactical Fighter Wing completes its redeployment from Ubon, Thailand.

The F–15 Eagle, a heavily armed air superiority fighter with a top speed of more than 900 mph, became operational in January 1976.

30 August: A C–5 Galaxy completes its first long-range air-refueled mission over water. Flying from Dover AFB, Delaware, to Clark AB, the aircraft covers 10,600 statute miles (via mid-Pacific routing) in 21 hours, 30 minutes.

30–31 August: Detachment 13, 41st Air Rescue and Recovery Wing, saves 36 Koreans from flood waters surrounding Kwangju, South Korea.

1 September: Maj James V. Sullivan and Maj Noel Widdifield set a New York to London speed record of 1,806.964 mph in a Lockheed SR–71A Blackbird aircraft.

3 September: SAC removes from alert its last Minuteman I ICBM at the 90th Strategic Missile Wing, Warren AFB, during the wing's conversion to Minuteman III missiles.

12 September: The United States returns the Takhli AB to the Royal Thai government.

24 October: The Space and Missile Systems Organization successfully launches a Minuteman I ICBM from a C–5A Galaxy cargo aircraft.

24 November: President Ford and Soviet General Secretary Leonid I. Brezhnev sign the Vladivostok SAL Accord. SAL limits deployment of both strategic delivery vehicles and multiple, independently targetable reentry vehicles.

December: Random operation of a balloon-borne radar (Seek Skyhook) begins at Cudjoe Key, Florida. It will keep watch on the Florida Strait between Cuba and the United States.

1 December: USAF directs the consolidation of TAC airlift resources with those of MAC.

18 December: President Ford signs a law allowing nonflyers to command flying units.

23 December: The first flight of a B–1 Lancer aircraft is made from Palmdale, California, to Edwards AFB.

1975

11 January: USAF cargo aircraft begins airlifting military equipment and supplies into Phnom Penh, Cambodia, which is under siege by communist forces.

13 January: The Secretary of the Air Force, Dr. John L. McLucas, selects the General Dynamics YF–16 prototype as USAF's air combat fighter, a low-cost, light-weight, highly maneuverable fighter aircraft.

16 January–1 February: Majs Roger J. Smith, David W. Peterson, and Willard R. MacFarlane set eight time-to-climb records in the F–15 Eagle, to earn the Mackay Trophy.

16 February: Brig Gen Eugene D. Scott becomes the first USAF navigator to command a flying unit by assuming command of the 47th Air Division, Fairchild AFB, Washington.

March–June: Air Rescue and Recovery Service personnel assist in the recovery of bodies and equipment from the wreckage of a C–141 Starlifter aircraft that crashed in the Olympic Mountains, Washington, on 21 March 1975.

5 March: Students fly the last T–29 navigator training sortie at Mather AFB.

25 March: The United States organizes an airlift to evacuate about 10,000 people a day from Da Nang, South Vietnam.

Communist forces surround and completely cut off this provincial city.

29 March: The United States begins an emergency airlift of military supplies and equipment into Saigon, South Vietnam.

31 March: Completing the consolidation of military airlift into one command, the tactical airlift resources of USAF's overseas commands (Pacific Air Forces, United States Air Forces in Europe, and Alaskan Air Command) transfer to MAC.

April: Just prior to the fall of the South Vietnamese government, MAC evacuates 50,493 refugees from Saigon, South Vietnam, to safe-haven bases in the Pacific.

4 April: The first USAF aircraft evacuating Vietnamese orphans from Saigon, South Vietnam, crash-lands shortly after takeoff. The heroic efforts of the flight and medical crews save the lives of 176 of the 314 passengers on the crashed C–5 Galaxy.

10 April: The B–1 Lancer aircraft attains supersonic flight speed for the first time.

12 April: American aircraft participate in Eagle Pull, the evacuation of United States personnel from Phnom Penh, Cambodia.

18 April: SAC begins transferring air refueling wings to the Air Force Reserve and Air National Guard. AFRES and ANG tanker units will support SAC alert operations.

21 April: SAC conducts its first in-flight refueling of the B–1 Lancer bomber.

29 April–16 September: During Operation New Arrival, 251 C–141 Starlifter and 349 commercial aircraft missions bring 121,562 Indochinese refugees to the United States from Pacific staging areas.

29–30 April: During Operation Frequent Wind, the final evacuation of Saigon, South Vietnam, USAF, U.S. Marine Corps, and U.S. Navy aircraft extract over 7,000 people as communist forces overrun the city.

12 May: Cambodian gunboats seize the U.S. merchant ship *Mayaguez* near the Wai Islands, 60 miles from the

Cambodian coast. In response, MAC airlifts Marines and equipment from the Philippines and Okinawa to Thailand.

14 May: Cambodia returns the *Mayaguez* crew after U.S. forces capture the ship and assault Koh Tang Island where the crew is thought to have been taken. Maj Robert W. Undorf is awarded the Mackay Trophy for conspicuous gallantry, initiative, and resourcefulness during this military operation.

6 June: The last 16 B–52 Stratofortress aircraft remaining at U-Tapao, Thailand, begin their redeployment to the United States.

15 June: The last F–111 unit in Thailand begins to redeploy to the United States.

17 June: Detachment 5, 37th Air Rescue and Recovery Squadron, saves 131 flood victims during a flood in a 13-county area of Montana.

1 July: The first ANG air refueling squadron begins supporting SAC operations. ANG and AFRES units will receive KC–135s over a four-year period.

7 August: Two C–141 Starlifter aircraft fly from Ramstein AB, Germany, to Bucharest, Romania, with disaster relief supplies requested by the Romanian government after extensive flooding of the Danube River tributaries.

1 September: Gen Daniel "Chappie" James Jr. becomes the first black officer to achieve four-star rank in the United States military.

29 October: The first F–5E Tiger II aircraft is delivered to Nellis AFB and takes its place in the USAF inventory.

29 November: The first Red Flag exercise begins at Nellis AFB ushering in a new era of highly realistic air combat training for USAF pilots.

1976

9 January: The USAF's first operational F–15 Eagle, the new air superiority fighter aircraft, arrives at 1st Tactical Fighter Wing, Langley AFB.

Daniel "Chappie" James poses in front of his F–4 during a break in the action in Vietnam. James became the first black officer in the United States military to attain four-star rank.

19 January: The 180th Tactical Fighter Group becomes the first ANG unit to participate in the Red Flag training program at Nellis AFB.

31 January: Udorn Royal Thai AB formally reverts to Thai control, the USAF having operated the base since October 1964.

5 February–3 March: Providing earthquake relief, MAC airlifts workers, emergency equipment, and supplies to Guatemala.

29 February: Korat Royal Thai AB lowers its American flag for the last time, marking termination of USAF operations at that base.

1 March: Taipei Air Station (AS), Taiwan, officially closes, ending 20 years of U.S. operation.

21–31 March: When a typhoon strikes Guam, C-5 Galaxy, C-141 Starlifter, and C-130 Hercules aircraft fly engineering teams, generators, utility vehicles, and communications equipment to the island.

22 March: The first A-10 Thunderbolt is delivered to Davis-Monthan AFB for operational test and evaluation.

22 March: A U-2 departing U-Tapao Airfield, Thailand, becomes the last SAC aircraft to leave Southeast Asia.

1 April: USAFE activates the 527th Tactical Fighter Aggressor Squadron at RAF Alconbury, United Kingdom, to conduct dissimilar air combat tactics training for fighter and reconnaissance aircrews.

2 April: The last C-118A Liftmaster in the active inventory is delivered to the Davis-Monthan AFB storage facility.

29 April–15 May: USAFE crews take part in the first Allied Air Forces Central Europe Tactical Weapons meet at Twenthe AB, the Netherlands.

6 May–5 June: In response to a devastating earthquake in the Furili region of northeastern Italy, USAF personnel at Aviano AB provide medical assistance and working parties to clear rubble and pitch tents for the homeless.

13 May–1 June: In the wake of Typhoons Olga and Pamela, Air Rescue and Recovery Service helicopters save 734 Philippine flood victims.

7–24 June: The first Team Spirit exercise, a joint/combined field training exercise, takes place in Korea. The primary purpose of the exercise, which in future years will expand to become the largest field training exercise in the free world, is to exercise, test, and evaluate the Korean tactical air control system.

27 June: The first successful test flight of a Titan II ICBM equipped with a universal space guidance system takes place at Vandenberg AFB.

28 June: The U.S. Air Force Academy becomes the first of the big three service academies to admit women cadets when it admits Joan Olsen.

15 July: Consolidated interservice navigation training begins for Navy and Marine personnel at Mather AFB.

27 July: Majs Adolphus H. Bledsoe Jr., pilot, and John T. Fuller, reconnaissance systems officer, fly an SR–71 Blackbird at a speed of 2,092.29 mph over a 1,000-kilometer (621.4 mile) course in the vicinity of Edwards AFB. In this flight, they set three closed-circuit records: (1) world absolute speed; (2) world jet speed with 1,000-kilogram (2,200 pounds) payload; and (3) world jet speed without payload.

28 July: Capt Eldon W. Joersz, pilot, and Maj George T. Morgan, reconnaissance systems officer, flying their SR–71 Blackbird at a speed of 2,193.64 mph, set two records: world absolute and jet speed over a 15/25-kilometer straight course.

28 July: Capt Robert C. Helt, pilot, and Maj Lang A. Elliot, reconnaissance systems officer, fly their SR–71 Blackbird to a height of 85,069 feet over the test range at Edwards AFB and establish both world absolute and jet records for altitude in horizontal flight.

1–2 August: Two USAF UH–1 Iroquois helicopter crews save 81 persons stranded by a flash flood in Colorado's Big Thompson Canyon.

20 August: Following a tree-cutting incident in which North Koreans kill two American Army officers, C–5 Galaxy and C–141 Starlifter aircraft airlift air and ground crewmen into Kunsan AB, Taegu AB, and Osan AB, South Korea.

6 September: A Soviet pilot lands his MiG–25 Foxbat jet fighter in Hokkaido, Japan, and asks for asylum in the United States. Japanese and United States officials closely examine the aircraft and then return it, dismantled, to the Soviet Union on 15 November.

16 September: The United States officially returns Eniwetok Atoll, site of the first U.S. hydrogen bomb explosion, to its former inhabitants.

29 September: The first of two groups of ten women-pilot candidates enter undergraduate pilot training at Williams AFB, Arizona, the first time since World War II that women could train to become pilots of military aircraft.

29 November: Responding to an earthquake disaster, MAC airlifts supplies and support equipment to various locations in Turkey.

8 December: The maiden flight of the full-scale development version of the F–16 Fighting Falcon is accomplished at Fort Worth, Texas.

CHRONOLOGY

1977–1986

1977

8 January: The first YC–141B (stretched C–141A Starlifter) rolls out of the Lockheed-Georgia Marietta plant. It is 23.3 feet longer than the original C–141A and capable of in-flight refueling.

11 February: After a heavy snowfall cripples Buffalo, New York, MAC airlifts approximately 995 tons of snow removal equipment and 495 passengers into Niagara Falls, New York, for snow cleanup operations.

18 February: The space shuttle makes its first captive flight atop the carrier aircraft, a modified Boeing 747.

1 March: The first three F–111Fs arrive in Europe and are assigned to the 48th Tactical Fighter Wing at RAF Lakenheath, United Kingdom.

10 March: The first woman navigator candidates report to Mather AFB to begin undergraduate navigator training.

23 March: TAC's first E–3A Sentry aircraft arrives at Tinker AFB, Oklahoma. The Sentry is an AWACS aircraft.

26 March–11 April: During Exercise Team Spirit '77, 548 aircraft from U.S. Air Force, U.S. Navy, U.S. Marine Corps, and Republic of Korea air force fly approximately 6,400 sorties.

30 March: Following the collision of a KLM 747 and a Pan Am 747 at Tenerife, Canary Islands, MAC C–130 Hercules and C–141 Starlifter aircraft transport more than 50 crash victims to McGuire AFB, New Jersey; Kelly AFB; Travis AFB; and El Toro Naval AS, California.

2 May: 1st Lt Christine E. Schott becomes the first woman undergraduate pilot training student to solo in the T–38 talon.

19 May: Capt James A. Yule is awarded the Mackay Trophy for gallantry and unusual presence of mind while participating in a flight as an instructor pilot of a B–52 Stratofortress aircraft.

19 June: A MAC C–5 Galaxy flies nonstop from Chicago–O'Hare Airport to Sheremetyevo Airport in Moscow carrying a 40-ton superconducting magnet, the first time a C–5 has landed in the Soviet Union. The 5,124-nautical-mile flight requires two aerial refuelings.

30 June: President James E. Carter announces the cancellation of the B–1 Lancer bomber production.

3 August: Cadet First Class Edward A. Rice Jr. of Yellow Springs, Ohio, becomes the first African-American commander of the Cadet Wing at the United States Air Force Academy.

4 August: The last T–33 Shooting Star leaves the Air Force Flight Test Center for retirement at Davis-Monthan AFB.

15 August: An Air Force Reserve Wing deploys two C–130B Hercules aircraft to California where they make 38 fire-retardant drops on four major forest fires.

2 September: The first class of women pilots graduates at Williams AFB.

3 September: The last of USAF stocks of Agent Orange from the Vietnam War are incinerated at sea, west of Johnston Island.

30 September: The first C–141 Starlifter transatlantic mission without a navigator aboard is flown from Charleston AFB, South Carolina, to Rota Naval Station, Spain. The mission uses the Delco inertial navigation system.

12 October: The first class of five USAF women navigators graduates, with three of the five assigned to MAC aircrews.

30 November: Control of Tachikawa AB is returned to the government of Japan.

6 December: As part of USAFE's survivability program, the first contingency launch and recovery airfield is completed at Hahn AB.

1978

January: A MAC C–141 Starlifter aircraft carries U.S. Department of Energy people and equipment to Edmonton, Alberta, Canada, to aid in the search for radioactive remains

A Minuteman III missile begins its flight downrange after launch from Cape Canaveral Air Force Station, Florida.

of a Soviet satellite that reentered the earth's atmosphere and disintegrated over the Canadian wilderness.

24 January: TAC deploys eight F-15 Eagle aircraft from Langley AFB to Osan AB. This is the first operational training deployment of the F-15s to the Western Pacific.

22 February: The first test NAVSTAR global positioning satellite successfully launches into orbit.

25–26 February: A MAC C-141 Starlifter transports 12 burn specialists from Newark, New Jersey, to the Waverly,

Tennessee, area following the explosion of a railway tank car filled with propane.

19 March: For the first time, USAFE F–15 Eagle and U.S. Navy Tomcat aircraft begin joint dissimilar air combat tactics training.

23 March: Capt Sandra M. Scott, a KC–135 Stratotanker pilot, becomes the first woman tanker commander to perform alert duty for SAC.

Capt Sandra M. "Sandy" Scott, the first woman tanker pilot to perform alert duty for Strategic Air Command.

The Titan II crew consisted of four missilemen: two officers and two enlisted people who controlled the launch and routine operations. Women first served on Titan crews in 1978.

May–June: After Katangan rebels invade Zaire's Shaba province from Angola, one C–5 Galaxy and 42 C–141 Starlifters airlift 931 tons of cargo and fuel and 124 passengers to Zaire to support Belgian and French operations there.

20–23 May: Lt Col Robert F. Schultz and crew and Capt Todd H. Hohberger and crew overcome the hazards of fatigue, limited en route support, crippling mechanical problems, and adverse operational conditions in a hostile area during delivery of supplies to Zaire. The C-5 crews will receive the Mackay Trophy for their achievement.

12 July: After 25 years of service to the nation, the last Boeing KC–97L Stratofreighter is retired to the Military Aircraft Storage and Disposition Center.

14–16 August: As part of the flood relief operations, a C–141 Starlifter delivers 26 tons of supplies to Khartoum, Sudan.

17 August: USAF accepts the first production model F–16 Fighting Falcon in a ceremony at the General Dynamics plant at Fort Worth, Texas.

18 August: AFC Tina M. Ponzer, assigned to the 381st Strategic Missile Wing, McConnell AFB, Kansas, becomes the first enlisted woman to perform maintenance on the Titan II ICBM.

24 August: The first three A–10 Thunderbolt aircraft assigned to USAFE arrive at RAF Bentwaters/Woodbridge, United Kingdom, for service with the 81st Tactical Fighter Wing.

24 August: Nitrogen tetroxide oxidizer leaking from a Stage I booster disables Titan II launch complex 533-7, assigned to the 381st Strategic Missile Wing, McConnell AFB. The escaped oxidizer kills two people and also severely damages the ICBM that is housed within the complex.

26 August: The Laotian government in Vientiane returns the remains of four U.S. servicemen killed in the Vietnam War, the first such gesture by Laos.

16 September: 1st Lt Patricia M. Fornes with the 381st SMW is the first woman officer to stand Titan II alert.

23 October: Two UH–1N Iroquois helicopters and one O–2A aircraft of the 24th Composite Wing fly flood-assistance missions in Costa Rica.

22 November: A C–141 Starlifter transports six medical specialists and their equipment from Boston, Massachusetts, to Algiers, Algeria, to aid the critically ill president of Algeria.

28 November: MAC C–141 Starlifter aircraft transport 911 bodies from the mass suicide at Jonestown, Guyana, to the military mortuary at Dover AFB.

30 November: The last Boeing Minuteman III ICBM is delivered to the USAF at Hill AFB, Utah.

9 December: As a result of political tensions and disturbances in Iran, MAC, using C–5 Galaxy and C–141 Starlifter aircraft, moves approximately 900 dependents from Teheran to locations in Europe and the United States.

1979

26 January: The first F–16 Fighting Falcon aircraft produced under the European participating government program is turned over to the Belgian air force.

29 January: E–3A Sentry aircraft assume a continental air defense mission responsibility.

31 March: Maj James E. McArdle Jr. receives the Mackay Trophy for professional competence and aerial skill in rescuing 28 Taiwanese seamen from a sinking cargo ship.

31 March: MAC aircraft fly the first of 15 missions to aid in activities following the 28 March accident at the Three-Mile Island nuclear power plant in Pennsylvania.

3–5 April: Two C–141 Starlifter aircraft move 21 tons of relief supplies to Nandi International Airport, Fiji, after Typhoon Meli batters the islands.

13 April: To aid undernourished and starving people, a C–141 Starlifter delivers 20 tons of vegetable seeds to Kamina, Zaire.

19–20 April: Following a major earthquake that struck the Adriatic coast of southern Yugoslavia and Albania, MAC delivers 139 tons of supplies and equipment to Titograd International Airport, Yugoslavia.

2–3 May: Two E–3A Sentry aircraft fly the first AWACS training mission over the central region in Europe.

1 June: The Community College of the Air Force moves from the Lackland Training Annex, Texas, to Maxwell AFB.

1 June: In support of SAC air tanker operations, USAFE activates RAF Fairford, United Kingdom. The base becomes fully operational with the arrival of two KC–135 Stratotanker aircraft on 12 September 1979.

5 June: President Carter approves full-scale development of the MX missile.

8–16 July: SAC conducts its first Global Shield '79, at the time the most comprehensive nuclear war plan exercise ever conducted.

4 September: Hurricane David precipitates aircraft evacuation from several TAC bases.

26 October: McDonnell Douglas terminates the F/RF–4 Phantom production line.

19–21 October: Two C–141 Starlifter aircraft equipped for aeromedical evacuation transport 38 severely burned U.S. marines from Yokota AB to Kelly AFB following a fire that swept through an enlisted men's barracks at a U.S. Marine Corps base at Mount Fuji, Japan.

2–21 December: In the aftermath of Typhoon Abby, MAC transports 250 support personnel and 650 tons of food, water purification equipment, and other supplies to the Marshall Islands International Airport, Majuro Atoll.

1980

2–4 January: The Portuguese government requests U.S. assistance for victims of an earthquake on Terceira Island in the Azores. Two C–141s of the 437th Military Airlift Wing provide 700 tents and 1,000 blankets for the homeless.

10–11 January: After Cyclone Claudette hits the Indian Ocean island of Mauritius just before New Year's day 1980, a C–141 from the 86th Military Airlift Squadron flew 17 tons of emergency supplies to the island. This humanitarian mission provided relief for thousands of homeless and destitute persons.

31 January: Construction workers inadvertently damage the aviation fuel pipeline between Clark AB and Subic Bay in the Philippines, causing the loss of approximately 50,000 gallons.

25–28 February: F–15s out of Clark AB intercept two Soviet Bear D and two Soviet Bear F aircraft after they penetrate the Philippine air defense interceptor zone.

26 February: PACAF hosts and participates in the first multinational exercise, Rimpac '80, that includes Japan. The exercise is held in Hawaiian waters.

12–14 March: Two B–52s from the 644th Bombardment Squadron and the 410th Bombardment Wing fly nonstop around the world in 43.55 hours, averaging 488 mph over 21,256 statute miles, to locate the Soviet navy operating in the Arabian Sea. For this accomplishment, the aircrews are awarded the Mackay Trophy.

31 March: USAF returns the facilities at Naha AB, Okinawa, to Japan. Included were 430 sets of family quarters and 226 acres of land.

6 April: The stretched C–141B flies its first operational mission. An aircrew from the 443d Military Airlift Wing flies it nonstop from Beale AFB to RAF Mildenhall in 11 hours, 12 minutes with only one aerial refueling.

7 April: Reacting to the Iranian seizure of the U.S. Embassy in Teheran, DOD orders all Iranian military trainees to leave the United States by 1200 hours on 11 April. Numerous Iranians enrolled in Air Training Command academic courses are expelled.

18 April: The Western Test Range building at Vandenberg AFB adds a $3 million Data Transfer Center to support the space shuttle, missile testing, and the global positioning system (GPS) navigational satellite network.

Night photo shot by approaching F–111F attack planes shows Soviet-made Il–76 transport aircraft at Tripoli Airport. The Aardvarks were equipped with the Pave Tack laser-designation targeting system.

22 April: Elements of the 33d ARRS stationed at both Clark AB and Kadena AB assist in the attempted rescue of 900 passengers from a ferry that sank approximately 150 statute miles southeast of Manila.

24 April: The attempt to rescue U.S. citizens being held as hostages in Teheran is halted when an RH–53 collides with an Air Force HC–130 in a sandstorm at a refueling site in the Iranian desert.

May: 2d Lt Mary L. Wittick is the first woman to enter the Air Force undergraduate helicopter pilot training program in Class 81-05.

18 May–5 June: Following eruptions of the Mount Saint Helens volcano in northwest Washington state, ARRS, Military Airlift wings, and the 9th Strategic Reconnaissance Wing conduct humanitarian relief efforts that include reconnaissance by two SR–71 Blackbirds.

28 May: For the first time, 97 women are among those receiving commissions as second lieutenants in graduation ceremonies at the United States Air Force Academy.

10 July–3 October: Operation Proud Phantom is the first tactical deployment in Egypt by the U.S. Air Force. The exercise begins with the arrival of 12 F–4Es in Cairo, Egypt, flown from Moody AFB.

28–30 July: A flight of four F–4E Phantoms from the 3d Tactical Fighter Wing, Clark AFB, flies to Tengah AB, Singapore. This is the first visit by USAF tactical aircraft to Singapore since the city-state achieved independence in 1965.

30 July–1 August: The 146th and 433d Tactical Airlift Wings respond with three C–130s and 10,500 gallons of fire retardant chemicals to quell seven brush fires near Palm Springs, California, in the San Bernardino National Forest. The airlift permits firefighters to bring the fire under control within three days.

7–16 August: The U.S. Air Force Southern Air Division flies 61 tons of relief equipment and a 107-person clean-up crew to assist the victims of Hurricane Allen in Haiti and Saint

Lucia, which killed at least 57 people and left hundreds homeless.

14 August: The first flight of the C–5A with modified wings occurs at Dobbins AFB. Lockheed-Georgia is contracted to retrofit 77 C–5As with new wings by July 1987.

2 September: An Air Weather Service detachment is activated at the Johnson Space Center, Houston, Texas, to advise space shuttle personnel of environmental issues and provide meteorological support during orbital flight tests.

10 September: An HH–3E from Osan AB rescues 229 people from the swirling waters of the Sea of Japan after Typhoon Orchid struck the eastern coast of South Korea southeast of Osan.

18 September: An explosion destroys the 308th Strategic Missile Wing's Titan II launch complex 374-7 in Little Rock, Arkansas. One Air Force maintenance person is killed.

20 September: PACAF sponsors visits by two F–15s and an E–3A to New Zealand, Malaysia, Singapore, and Thailand to demonstrate these new aircraft.

1 October: Operation Elf is initiated with four E–3As deployed to Riyadh, Saudi Arabia, to protect Saudi air space during the Iran-Iraq War.

3 October: Piloting an HH–3 Jolly Green Giant helicopter, Capt John J. Walters and two pararescuemen rescue 61 passengers and crew aboard the burning Dutch luxury liner *Prinsendam* 120 miles south of Yakutat, Alaska. Captain Walters wins the Mackay Trophy for his bravery.

12–23 October: On 10 October an earthquake registering 7.2 on the Richter scale and centered in the region of El Asnam, Algeria, kills some 6,000 people and leaves more than 100,000 homeless. The 322d Airlift Division, the 436th, 437th, and 438th Military Airlift Wings, and the 435th Tactical Airlift Wing transported more than 400 tons of relief supplies and 87 passengers on behalf of the Algerian victims.

17 October: The Secretary of Defense directs the U.S. Army to take over operations at Wheeler AFB although ownership of the base remains with PACAF. Since the reactivation of Wheeler in 1952, the Army has been the principal flying user of the base.

20–23 October: The U.S. Air Force Southern Air Division units fly 40 tons of food, medical supplies, and accessories to northwestern Nicaragua to succor flood victims.

12–14 November: For the first time, USAFE tasks an entire wing, the 50th Tactical Fighter, to exercise its wartime mission in a chemical environment for a sustained period. The training exercise is held at Hahn AB.

12–25 November: Rapid Deployment Force elements of USAFE represent the first joint overseas exercise in Egypt when they participate in Operation Bright Star.

20 November: The first F–111 Pave Tack-modified aircraft arrives at the 48th Tactical Fighter Wing, RAF Lakenheath, United Kingdom. The F–111 Pave Tack system provides a 24-hour high- and low-altitude weapons delivery capability.

21 November: Responding to a fire at the 26-story MGM Grand Hotel in Las Vegas, Nevada, all the 20th and 302d Special Operations Squadrons, as well as Detachment 1 of the 57th Fighter Weapons Wing, rescue 310 persons.

23 November–2 December: In the wake of a severe earthquake in the Naples area of southern Italy, USAFE provides logistical assistance, including 300 tons of tents, blankets, and medical supplies through the auspices of MAC. In close proximity to the disaster, the 2181st Communications Squadron at Monte Vergine, Italy, provides relief to the local communities that sustained damages.

25 November: The 26th Tactical Fighter Training Aggressor Squadron flies its final T–38 sortie. Replacing the four T–38 Talons after they are returned to the Air Training Command are F–5E and F–5F aircraft.

25–29 November: The outbreak of 11 major fires in a 125-square-mile area covering four counties east of Los Angeles, California, brings to the disaster scene units of MAC and the Air Force Airlift Readiness Center. Thirteen hundred and five tons of fire-retardant chemicals are sprayed on the fires.

10 December: Four E–3A AWACS aircraft are sent by USAFE to Ramstein AB to participate in Operation Elf, the ongoing cooperative effort with Saudi Arabia to monitor Middle Eastern airspace. In view of the crisis in Poland, an additional four E–3As are deployed to Europe.

12 December: After two and one-half years of study, the Community College of the Air Force at Maxwell AFB is accredited by the Commission on Colleges of the Southern Association to award the Associate in Applied Science degree.

1981

January–June: Operating from Corpus Christi, Texas, and Little Rock, Arkansas, MAC C–130 Hercules deliver 500 tons of arms, ammunition, helicopters, and other war materials worth $5 million to El Salvador. The operation assists the Salvadorian government in its operations against leftist guerrillas.

11 January: Boeing Company delivers the first two air-launched cruise missiles to the 416th Bombardment Wing, Griffiss AFB, for initial use in environmental testing and maintenance training. Capable of delivering a nuclear weapon to a target 1,500 miles away, the ALCM contains a terrain-contour-matching feature allowing extremely low altitude flight to avoid detection by enemy radar.

12 January: Terrorists destroy nine A–7D Corsair aircraft assigned to the ANG 156th Tactical Fighter Group at Muniz ANG Base, Puerto Rico.

18–25 January: Two MAC C–9 Nightingales transport 52 Americans held by Iran for 444 days to Rhein-Main AB. After a four-day stay at the USAF hospital in Wiesbaden, Germany, the former hostages return to the United States via a MAC VC–137.

23 January: Two helicopters from the 6594th Test Group perform a pararescue-assisted hoist pickup of an injured seaman from a merchant vessel 240 nautical miles west of Honolulu, Hawaii.

10 February: Three U–1 helicopters from the 57th Fighter Weapons Wing at Indian Springs Air Force Auxiliary Field, Nevada, rescue nine guests trapped by fire on the roof of the 30-story Las Vegas Hilton. Firefighters from Nellis AFB help extinguish the flames.

28 February–6 March: After earthquakes strike central Greece, the 7206th Air Base Group at Hellenikon AB assists relief efforts with emergency supplies and equipment.

12 March: The Aerospace Defense Command selects Peterson AFB, Colorado, as the site for the backup facility to the North American Aerospace Defense (NORAD) Command, Cheyenne Mountain Complex. The facility will assume command and control functions should the NORAD Complex experience a failure during peacetime.

17 March: Douglas Aircraft Company delivers the first KC–10A Extender tanker/cargo aircraft to SAC. Substantially larger than the KC–135 tanker/cargo aircraft it supplements, the Extender carries advanced equipment enabling it to refuel a wide variety of aircraft while delivering cargo overseas.

18 March: The arrival of 80 F–15 Eagles at the 18th Tactical Fighter Wing completes the conversion of PACAF to the new fighter-bomber. The 18th Tactical Fighter Wing transfers 79 F–4 Phantoms to other commands.

12–15 April: USAF space tracking and communications systems operated by the Aerospace Defense Command and the Air Force Communications Command support the space shuttle's maiden flight.

14 June: Six F–15 Eagles from the 36th Tactical Fighter Wing and one from the 32d Tactical Fighter Wing become the first USAFE aircraft to participate in the TAC's Red Flag exercise.

July: Heavy rains cause widespread flooding south of Osan AB. USAF helicopters assigned to the 33d ARRS cooperate with the Republic of Korea forces to rescue 118 people from the rising waters.

3 August: USAF air traffic controllers man civilian U.S. airport facilities, replacing striking personnel. Thanks to military assistance, civilian air operations continue service despite the strike.

14 September: The first operational F–16 Fighting Falcons of PACAF arrive at Kunsan AB. At the end of the year, 34 operational aircraft are located there.

15 September: SAC receives its first TR–1A reconnaissance aircraft. Built by Lockheed-California, this improved and enlarged version of the U–2 reconnaissance aircraft can conduct all-weather day and night operations at altitudes exceeding 70,000 feet.

21 September: ARRS helicopters based at Clark AB cooperate with the U.S. Navy and Philippine authorities to rescue 18 of 97 crew members from the grounded Philippine navy destroyer *Datu Kalantiaw*. This event increases the total for individuals rescued by ARRS to 20,000 during 35 years of service.

1 October: Air Training Command begins a special program at Mather AFB to train German weapon system officers for duty in the second seat of the Tornado fighter-bomber, a two-seat, swing-wing aircraft similar to the F–111 fighter-bomber.

2 October: Reversing President Carter's decision to end the B–1 Lancer program, President Ronald Reagan announces that the Air Force will build and deploy 100 of these aircraft. President Reagan also announces that the M–X missile will initially be deployed in existing missile silos.

2 October: Deputy Secretary of Defense Frank P. Carlucci orders the inactivation of the Titan II weapon system. This decision ends several years of controversy surrounding the viability and safety of the United States's largest ICBM.

14 October: The TAC deploys two E–3A Sentry AWACS aircraft to Egypt to help ensure calm after the assassination of Prime Minister Anwar Sadat.

21 October: The Euro–North Atlantic Treaty Organization Joint Jet Pilot Training Program begins at Sheppard AFB. Modeled after the undergraduate pilot training program conducted for the German air force since 1966, this program trains pilots from Belgium, Canada, Denmark, Germany, Greece, Italy, the Netherlands, Norway, Portugal, Turkey, the United Kingdom, and the United States.

5 November: The first operational EF–111A defense suppression aircraft is delivered to the 388th Electronic Combat Squadron at Mountain Home AFB, Idaho. The EF–111A will eventually replace EB–66 and EB–57 aircraft to provide worldwide support of tactical air strike forces.

23 November: During the Bright Star '82 exercise, eight B–52 bombers assigned to the strategic projection force establish a record for the longest nonstop B–52 bombing mission. Flying a distance of 15,000 miles with three midair refuelings in 31 hours from air bases in North Dakota, the bombers deliver their conventional munitions on a simulated runway in Egypt.

31 December: Following the arrival of training models in mid-September, the first operational F–16 assigned to USAFE arrives at the 50th Tactical Fighter Wing, Hahn AB.

1982

26 January: Maj Gen Michael Collins (USAF Reserve), one of the three crew members on the *Apollo XI* mission to the moon, flies his last mission as a reserve officer in an F–16 Fighting Falcon aircraft at Edwards AFB.

28 January: The first of 76 C–5 Galaxy aircraft to receive new wings is delivered to Lockheed-Georgia. Modification of these aircraft is expected to cost $1.4 bilion.

24 February: The airborne early warning force at Geilenkirchen NATO AB, Germany, receives its first of 18 authorized E–3A Sentry aircraft.

3 March: The initial flight of six A–10 Thunderbolt aircraft arrives at Suwon AB, South Korea. The Republic of Korea will build more than 50 facilities totaling over 700,000 square feet to support the A–10 beddown project, known as Commando Vulcan.

24 March: USAFE acquires Comiso AS, Sicily, as a ground-launch cruise missile site.

4–8 May: An E–3A Sentry AWACS aircraft deploys for the first time to Turkey.

30 May: Spain, long a host to USAF bases, joins NATO.

10 June: SAC's first all-woman KC-135 crew, assigned to the 924th Air Refueling Squadron, Castle AFB, perform a five-hour training mission that includes a midair refueling of a B–52 Stratofortress aircraft.

14 June: The 313th Tactical Fighter Squadron, Hahn AB, becomes the first F–16 Fighting Falcon operationally ready squadron in USAFE.

21 June: SAC's tanker operations attain another level of success with an aerial refueling 750 miles north of the South Pole. While establishing the record for the southernmost in-flight refueling, the KC–10A Extender transfers 67,400 pounds of aviation fuel during the rendezvous in support of MAC resupply operations in Antarctica, the largest amount ever.

1 July: USAFE activates the first of six ground-launched cruise missile (GLCM) wings to be stationed in Europe, the 501st TMW, at RAF Greenham Common, United Kingdom.

2 July: SAC phases out its first Titan II missile, removing from alert the missile assigned to Site 9 at the 570th Strategic Missile Squadron, Davis-Monthan AFB.

6–13 July: A C–130 Hercules aircraft airlifts 113 tons of sorghum and vegetable oil to refugees in Africa during the Chadian civil war.

15 July: SAC launches its 1,500th missile from Vandenberg AFB. The tests at Vandenberg date from 15 December 1958.

30 August: The F–5G (later, F–20) Tigershark makes its first flight at Edwards AFB.

2 September: B–1B prototype no. 4 lands at Farnborough, England. Its 11.4-hour nonstop flight from Edwards AFB marks the first landing of a B–1 aircraft at a site other than Edwards AFB.

16 September: Capt Ron Cavendish and crew E-21 successfully land their B-52 Stratofortress after the aircraft lost both of its rudder elevator hydraulic systems. This feat had never before been accomplished without significant damage to or complete destruction of the aircraft. The crew is slated to receive the Mackay Trophy.

21 September: A B-52 Stratofortress of the 416th Bombardment Wing, Griffiss AFB, conducts the first air-launched cruise missile operational test.

23 September: Headquarters USAF activates Space Command, later to be designated Air Force Space Command.

14–19 November: The 527th Tactical Fighter Training Aggressor Squadron deploys three F-5 Tiger aircraft to Eskisehir AB, Turkey, for its first dissimilar air combat tactics training with the Turkish air force.

16 November: The space shuttle Columbia completes its first operational flight (and fifth overall) when it lands on runway 22 at Edwards AFB. With a crew of four, it becomes the first spacecraft ever to ferry more than three people into space.

16 December: The 416th Bombardment Wing at Griffiss AFB places the first air-launched cruise missile on alert.

24–30 December: MAC airlifts 87 tons of supplies (tents, blankets, medical supplies, and generators) to earthquake victims in the Yemen Arab Republic. The earthquake struck on 13 December.

1983

1 January: United States Central Command is activated at MacDill AFB, Florida, as a unified command. This will be Gen H. Norman Schwarzkopf's command in Desert Storm in January 1991.

February: A C-141 Starlifter transports 15 tons of communications equipment from the United States to Lagos, Nigeria, to restore disrupted services when a fire destroys a telecommunications center.

1 February: Ahuas Tara I, a combined, joint training exercise that involves many USAF units, commences in Honduras. It demonstrates American support for noncommunist regimes in Central America and puts pressure on neighboring Nicaragua, which is aligned with Cuba and the Union of Soviet Socialist Republics (USSR).

1 February: The 868th Tactical Missile Training Squadron begins training personnel to operate GLCMs scheduled to be deployed in Europe.

2 February: F–16 Fighting Falcon pilot training begins at Luke AFB.

3 February: In an effort to modernize America's retaliatory capability, SAC completes retrofitting 300 Minuteman III ICBMs with new reentry systems.

1 March: MAC activates the Twenty-third Air Force at Scott AFB, Illinois, to provide combat rescue, special operations, weather reconnaissance, atmospheric sampling, security support for missile sites, training of USAF helicopter and HC–130 crewmen, and pararescue training.

1 March: The 1st Special Operations Wing is reassigned from TAC to MAC. Hurlburt Field, Florida, is also reassigned from TAC to MAC.

15–28 March: SAC successfully demonstrates three launches of AGM–84 Harpoon missiles from B–52 Stratofortresses at the Pacific Missile Test Range, Kwajalein Atoll. The command is exploring its ability to perform sea interdiction missions.

1 April–1 May: USAF transfers 31 SAC units and four installations to Space Command, which takes over missile warning and space surveillance systems.

1–8 April: An American C–130 Hercules transport aircraft airlifts at least 34 tons of shelters, medical supplies, electric generators, and floodlights from Panama to victims of an earthquake in southwestern Colombia.

5–10 April: Up to 20 inches of rain falls over southeastern Louisiana, flooding the state penitentiary and 40,000 homes. Four USAF C–141 Starlifter aircraft airlift 83 tons of tents, cots, field kitchens, and other relief cargo.

26 April: The first GLCM training class graduates at Davis-Monthan AFB and its personnel are assigned to a TMW in USAFE.

1 May: USAF begins flying surveillance missions over the Bahamas to help local police apprehend drug smugglers.

17 June: The first Peacekeeper ICBM, carrying multiple warheads, is launched at Vandenberg AFB. The unarmed warheads land in the Kwajalein target area in the Pacific Ocean.

26 June–1 July: Three USAF C–130 Hercules aircraft transport 170 tons of food, medicine, and other relief supplies to the victims of a flood in northwestern Peru.

4 June: At Hill AFB F–105 Thunderchiefs stage a final flyby to mark the phasing out of the last AFRES Thunderchief squadron.

1 July: A provisional USAF support squadron is activated at Riyadh AB, Saudi Arabia, as a war rages between Iran and Iraq, posing a threat to nearby Saudi Arabia and its oil-rich neighbors in the Persian Gulf.

24 July–6 August: Two USAF UH–1 helicopters transport medical personnel and ten tons of food and medical supplies to the victims of a flood in western Ecuador.

1 August: Six minutes after Air Force One lands at Andrews AFB with President Ronald Reagan aboard, a microburst with winds of 120 knots strikes the base, causing $465,000 worth of damage.

August: Three C–123 Providers of the 907th Tactical Airlift Group spray insecticide over 11 Minnesota counties to counter an encephalitis epidemic.

7 August: A terrorist bomb, possibly planted by antinuclear activists, explodes at the Officers Club at Hahn AB.

10 August: Secretary of Defense Caspar W. Weinberger directs the Air Force to deploy 100 Peacekeeper missiles in Minuteman silos.

15 August–15 September: Twelve C–141 Starlifter missions transport 185 tons of cargo to Chad in Africa as part of a security assistance program.

1 September: A Soviet SU–15 interceptor shoots down Korean Airline Flight 007, a Boeing 747 airliner with 269 people aboard, near Sakhalin Island north of Japan. Three HC–130 Hercules aircraft from the 33d ARRS at Kadena AB participate in subsequent search but find no survivors. SAC KC–135 Stratotankers support the search operation.

3–25 September: As part of Operation Rubber Wall, MAC flies 85 C–141 Starlifter, 24 C–5 Galaxy, and four C–130 Hercules missions to transport about 4,000 tons of supplies from the United States to American marines in Lebanon.

5 September: A KC–135 Stratotanker crew led by Capt Robert J. Goodman saves an F–4E Phantom and its crew over the Pacific. The KC–135 refuels the F–4E four times and tows it with a refueling boom. The crew receives the Mackay Trophy for the most meritorious flight of the year.

28 September: The Air Force designates the new EF–111A tactical electronic jamming aircraft as the Raven.

1 October: The last B–52D Stratofortresses are retired. This is the aircraft that flew most of the Arc Light bombing missions over Vietnam.

4–5 October: Four CH–3 helicopters of the 302d Special Operations Squadron transport 57 residents of the Maricopa area of Arizona to higher ground during a flood.

6 October: Three B–52G Stratofortress bombers are modified to carry the AGM–84 Harpoon antiship missile.

23 October–9 December: After a terrorist bomb explodes at the U.S. Marine barracks in Beirut, Lebanon, MAC and AFRES cargo and aeromedical evacuation aircraft transport 239 dead and 95 wounded Americans to the United States and Europe for burial and medical treatment.

25 October–2 November: In Operation Urgent Fury, American military forces invade the Caribbean island of Grenada to evacuate Americans threatened by a coup and to restore political stability. During the deployment phase, MAC and AFRES C–5 Galaxy, C–141 Starlifter, and C–130 Hercules aircraft fly 496 missions to transport 11,389

USAF aircraft drop Army paratroopers during Operation Urgent Fury, the invasion of Grenada in October 1983.

passengers and 7,709 tons of cargo. SAC tankers and TAC fighters, as well as ANG EC–130Es, also support the operation.

25 October–23 November 1984: During Urgent Fury, the military operation to protect American citizens on Grenada, Lt Col James L. Hobson Jr. leads a flight of MC–130 Hercules aircraft to successfully complete an airborne assault on Point Salinas. After dropping paratroopers at the exact planned time over target in a hail of 7.62 mm and 23 mm antiaircraft fire, Colonel Hobson dives the aircraft to 100 feet (air ground level) and departs the area. For his actions in assuming the assault lead from a disabled aircraft, Colonel Hobson receives the Mackay Trophy.

27 October: B–52 Stratofortresses deploy to Spain for the first time.

1–5 November: Four C–141 Starlifters and six C–130 Hercules transport 234 tons of tents, blankets, stoves, food, and clothing to the victims of a 30 October earthquake in northeastern Turkey.

23 November: The West German Parliament approves the deployment of USAF GLCMs and U.S. Army Pershing II ballistic missiles in Germany.

1 December: The Air Force ceases training of Titan II missile crews. The first of the Titan II units to be inactivated sees its demise the next day. SAC inactivates the 571st Strategic Missile Squadron, the first of the Titan II units to be inactivated, the next day.

6 December: The National Transonic Tunnel, a wind tunnel to test ultra-fast aircraft, is dedicated at Langley AFB.

23 December: The 390th Electronic Combat Squadron attains initial operational capability as the first EF–111A Raven unit.

1984

1 January: The Space Command assumes resource management of the GPS.

21 January: While conducting the first free-flight test of the antisatellite missile from an F–15 Eagle carrier, the missile deploys a dummy miniature-vehicle emulator.

28 January: The first F–16 Fighting Falcon is accepted by the AFRES at Hill AFB.

31 January: The AGM–81A Firebolt target vehicle sets a world speed and altitude record during its seventh development test and evaluation flight: Mach 4.1 and 103,000 feet.

3 February: The first USAFE EF–111A Raven electronic combat aircraft arrives at the 20th Tactical Fighter Wing, RAF Upper Heyford, United Kingdom.

23 February: The first F–15C Eagle is received by the TAC. The Eagle replaces the F–4 Phantom as the USAF's air-superiority fighter.

24 February: MAC flies two C–141 Starlifter missions from Larnaca, Cyprus, to Cherry Point, North Carolina, to support the withdrawal of U.S. Marines from Lebanon, as part of the multinational peacekeeping force.

6 March: A B–52G Stratofortress from the 319th Bombardment Wing conducts the first air-launched cruise missile captive-carry mission over Canada's Northern Test Range. In a related development on the same day, the federal court of Canada dismisses a suit seeking to end these tests.

19 March–9 April: MAC flies 28 C–5 Galaxy and 17 C–141 Starlifter missions and deploys an E–3A Sentry in support of Egypt and Sudan against threats from Libya.

6 April: The first Learjet C–21A aircraft is accepted by the 375th Aeromedical Airlift Wing on a contractual basis. It is the first of 80 Learjet aircraft delivered to the Air Force as replacements for the aging CT–39 Sabreliner aircraft.

11 April: The 375th Aeromedical Airlift Wing accepts its first contract Beech Aircraft Corporation C–12F. USAF will procure 40 new C–12Fs to be used for operational support airlift.

19 April: Ground-breaking ceremonies are held at Site III of the phased array, sea-launched ballistic missile warning system, Pave Paws, at Robins AFB.

16 May: MAC C–141 Starlifters deliver 22 tons of medical supplies to Afghan refugees at Peshawar, Pakistan.

25 May: A MAC C–141 Starlifter transports the body of the Unknown Soldier of the Vietnam War for interment at Arlington National Cemetery.

15 June: A MAC C–130 Hercules flies 4.5 tons of pumps and other equipment from Dyess AFB, Texas, to Kansas City, Missouri, to assist flood-fighting efforts in critical areas of northwest Missouri.

15 June: The first Peacekeeper with a Mark–21 test reentry vehicle is flight-tested at Vandenberg AFB.

20 June: After completion of a two-year operational test and evaluation program, Boeing transfers the first KC–135R Stratotanker aircraft to SAC's 384th Air Refueling Wing. The KC–135R, a KC–135A modified with CFM–56 engines, off-loads more fuel and is cheaper to operate and is quieter than the KC–135A.

21 June: A KC–10A Extender tanker from the 22d Air Refueling Wing, March AFB, California, operates for the first time from Christchurch International Airport, New Zealand, providing three air refuelings to a MAC C–141B Starlifter. This Starlifter is responsible for midwinter air-drop reprovisioning of the U.S. Antarctic bases at the South Pole and McMurdo Sound.

30 June: Hancock Field, New York, closes, ending 32 years of continuous operation.

July: The first Harpoon (AGM–84) antiship missile is delivered to the 69th Bombardment Squadron, 42d Bombardment Wing, Loring AFB.

31 July: The 570th Strategic Missile Squadron, Davis-Monthan AFB, is inactivated. Simultaneously, the 390th Strategic Missile Wing, Davis-Monthan AFB, becomes the first Titan II wing to be inactivated.

8 August: The first USAFE C–23 Sherpas enter USAF service in the European distribution system.

7 August–2 October: MAC supports the deployment of U.S. minesweeping assets to the Red Sea in response to Egyptian and Saudi Arabian concerns over mysterious underwater explosions that damaged ships.

19–20 August: Two C–141 Starlifters from the Twenty-second Air Force evacuate 382 American military and civilian personnel from Johnston Island in the face of Typhoon Kell. The atoll is located 715 miles from Hawaii. Storm winds in excess of 115 mph rip over the island, and waves crest to over 40 feet.

28 August: A C–5 Galaxy arrives at Florennes AB, Belgium, with the first shipment of support equipment for GLCMs.

29 August: The last USAFE OV–10 Broncos depart Sembach AB, Germany, for George AFB after a decade of operations in Europe.

2–3 September: Rescue units, including the 38th ARRS, log 148 saves in Korea during flood relief operations.

4 September: The first production Rockwell B–1B Lancer bomber rolls out at Air Force Plant 42 in Palmdale, California.

19–21 September: A C–141 Starlifter flies to Kinshasa, Zaire, to support AIDS research sponsored by the U.S. National Institute of Health.

11–14 October: MAC transports U.S. Secret Service vehicles assigned to protect Pope John Paul II during his visit to San Juan, Puerto Rico.

18 October: The B–1B Lancer conducts its first flight ahead of schedule.

18–20 October: The Air Force Rescue Coordination Center coordinates search and rescue missions, resulting in 47 saves during conditions of heavy snow, low temperatures, and high winds in Colorado and New Mexico.

23–24 October: One H–3 Jolly Green Giant helicopter from the 31st ARRS and a C–130 Hercules transport from the 374th Tactical Airlift Wing, Thirteenth Air Force, rescue nine persons trapped by fire on the roof of the Pines Hotel, Baguio, Republic of the Philippines, and transport 48 people injured to Clark AB for treatment. Victims were attending the 40th anniversary of Gen Douglas MacArthur's return to the Philippines during World War II at Leyte.

25 October: F–4E Phantoms participate in USAFE's 86th Tactical Fighter Wing's first joint, live-fire missile exercise with the U.S. Navy at the Salto di Quirra, off the east coast of Sardinia.

2 November: Fire erupts at McConnell AFB after liquid fuel is unloaded from a Titan II missile. The incident jeopardizes the Titan II deactivation schedule.

19 November: Two MAC C–141 Starlifters deliver six motor vehicles and a quantity of small arms ammunition to the U.S. Embassy at Bogota, Columbia, after drug dealers threaten the safety of American personnel in that country.

20 November: President Reagan approves formation of a new unified command, the United States Space Command.

1 December: The C–5A Galaxy enters service with the AFRES at Kelly AFB.

11–12 December: Two C–141 Starlifters fly survivors and two casualties of a Kuwaiti airlines aircraft hijacking to Rhein-Main AB and to the continental United States.

20 December: Two C–130 Hercules aircraft airlift 23.8 tons of emergency rescue equipment and vehicles to expedite the recovery of 27 coal miners trapped more than a mile beneath the earth's surface near Huntington, Utah. These four-wheel-drive vehicles enabled rescuers to reach the disaster site and recover the remains of the deceased miners, who had succumbed to carbon monoxide poisoning or smoke inhalation.

22 December–8 March 1985: Eight C–141 Starlifters carry over 212 tons of food, tents, water tanks, and medical supplies from Italy to Kassala, Sudan. This American relief effort is in response to the needs of 100,000 Ethiopian refugees fleeing from famine in Niger and Mali in the Sahel region of Africa.

1985

January: Headquarters SAC and Ogden Air Logistics Center determine that the 2 November 1984 fire at Launch Complex 532-7, 381st Strategic Missile Wing, McConnell AFB, was caused by a leakage preventable by procedural changes. This finding enables Titan II deactivation to proceed according to schedule.

1 January: Lt Col David E. Faught, a 97th Bombardment Wing instructor pilot, prevents the loss of a KC–135 Stratotanker and saves the lives of seven fellow crewmen. The aircraft's nose gear refuses to extend, and after 13 hours in the air attempting to fix the problem, Colonel Faught lands the aircraft with only minor equipment damage and no personal injuries. He receives the Mackay Trophy for his actions.

4 January: Maj Patricia M. Young becomes the first woman commander of an Air Force Space Command unit—Detachment 1, 20th Missile Warning Squadron.

5 January: A MAC C–141 Starlifter transports a Sikorsky S–70 helicopter to La Paz, Bolivia, to assist in the search for an Eastern Airlines Boeing 727 that crashed high in the Andes Mountains.

18–23 January: MAC C–141 Starlifters move 62 tons of cargo directly to the Sudan, relieving the plight of Ethiopian refugees.

19–21 January: Two C–5 Galaxies and one C–141 Starlifter from the 75th and 312th Military Airlift Squadrons transport 186 tons of supplies consisting of 2,400 tents, tarpaulins, plastic sheeting, and water trailers to Viti Levu Island, Fiji, to supply relief for victims of Typhoon Eric. The typhoon devastated Viti Levu, leaving 3,000 people homeless.

28 January: Two H–3 Jolly Green Giant helicopters rescue ten shipwrecked Korean fishermen. The survivors are airlifted to Kunsan AB for medical treatment.

3 February: MAC C–141 Starlifters transport 500 tents from Howard AB, Panama, to central Argentina after an earthquake destroys the homes of nearly 12,000 people.

An Air Force helicopter hoists a crew member off a wrecked boat near Okinawa. Throughout its life, the Air Force has played a major role in rescue missions for military people and civilians.

4 February: SAC authorizes the creation of gender-specific (all-male or all-female) missile launch crews for Minuteman and Peacekeeper. Previously, women served only with the Titan II weapon system, whose large launch-control facility ensured personal privacy.

5–9 March: Airlift crews fly 123 tons of food and medicine as part of four famine-relief missions to Sudan, Niger, and Mali.

8 March: MAC helicopters assist Bahamian police and U.S. Drug Enforcement Agency officials in confiscating 1,800 pounds of cocaine worth $320 million.

15 March: A MAC C–5 Galaxy delivers over 1,000 rolls of plastic sheeting used to create protective shelters for victims of an earthquake that ravaged coastal and interior regions of central Chile on 3 February 1985.

25 March: The Secretary of the Air Force announces changes in the combat-exclusion policy for women. Henceforth, women can serve as forward air controllers, fly and crew various models of the C–130 Hercules, and work in munitions storage facilities.

5 April: Two C–141 Starlifters and one C–130 Hercules aircraft from MAC transport 10.9 tons of fire-fighting equipment, 21,000 gallons of fire retardant, and 190 fire fighters to fight a blaze covering over 7,000 acres in the mountains of western North Carolina. Strong winds and drought conditions accelerate the fire to cover more than six counties of the state.

5–20 April: MAC provides helicopter support for Operation Bahamas and Turks, a joint United States–Commonwealth of the Bahamas operation to intercept drugs destined for the United States.

20 April: B–52 Stratofortress crews complete initial training for Harpoon antiship missile operations.

29 April–17 May: USAFE units assigned at Spangdahlem AB participate in Salty Demo, the first integrated basewide effort to measure all facets of an air base's ability to survive attacks and generate postattack sorties.

21 June–25 July: Three C–123K Provider aerial-spray-capable transports respond to the grasshopper infestation of public lands in southern Idaho. By spraying more than 735,000 acres in 73 sorties, the aircraft prevent locust damage to private croplands.

29 June: The 60th Bombardment Squadron, 43d Strategic Wing, from Andersen AFB becomes the second B–52G Stratofortress squadron to be equipped with the Harpoon antiship missile. This event marks the attainment of full operational capability for the weapon system.

30 June: AFSC conducts the final Peacekeeper test launch from the above-ground launch pad at Vandenberg AFB.

1 July: The 7th Bombardment Wing, Carswell AFB, becomes the first unit to receive air-launched cruise missiles modified for use on B–52H Stratofortress bombers.

1 July: A C–141 Starlifter from the 438th Military Airlift Wing transports 39 passengers released from Trans World Airlines flight 847, which was hijacked on 30 June by two Shiite Moslems. Upon arrival at Rhein-Main AB from Damascus, the survivors are greeted by Vice President George Bush.

2–10 July: C–141 Starlifters transport 285 fire fighters and 460 tons of flame retardant to help suppress forest fires in Idaho and California. C–130 Hercules aircraft fly 200 sorties, dropping fire retardant over an area exceeding 1.5 million acres.

7 July: The first operational B–1B Lancer is accepted by SAC and the 96th Bombardment Wing at Dyess AFB.

15 July: Two 42d Bombardment Wing B–52 Stratofortresses simulate Harpoon launches as part of United States Atlantic Command's exercise Readex '85-2. This event marks the first full operational test and evaluation of the Harpoon antiship missile.

30 July: The U.S. Air Force Bomarc (CQM–10B) aerial Target Drone Program ends.

12–15 August: A C–5A Galaxy from the 436th Military Airlift Wing responds to a State Department request to assist over 2 million flood and famine victims in Western Sudan and deliver 35 tons of equipment, including three helicopters.

23 August: AFSC successfully conducts America's first land-based "cold launch" from an underground silo, a modified Minuteman launch facility at Vandenberg AFB. The cold-launch technique ejects the missile from the silo by gas pressure, and the propellant ignites after it becomes airborne. As a result, only minimal damage to the silo results, greatly reducing the refurbishing time needed for another launch.

13 September: The first antisatellite intercept test takes place when an air-launched antisatellite weapon successfully destroys a resident space object, the Solwing scientific satellite.

21–30 September: Airlift units fly 375 tons of cargo to Mexico City following massive earthquakes.

11–12 October: A C–141 Starlifter of the 438th Military Airlift Wing flies the 11 released American survivors from the hijacked Italian cruise ship *Achille Lauro* from Cairo, Egypt, to Newark, New Jersey.

15 October: The first flight of the T–46A Next Generation Trainer occurs at Edwards AFB.

16 October: Two H–3 Jolly Green Giant helicopters, supported by two refueling-capable HC–130 Hercules aircraft, rescue 33 shipwrecked survivors of the Philippine ship *Marcos Faberes*.

1 November: The Dutch approve deployment of USAFE GLCMs at Woensdrecht, the Netherlands.

4 November: Air Force Rescue Coordination Center coordinates missions that save 47 lives during flood-relief operations in the Shenandoah Valley, Virginia.

15–18 November: USAF airlifts 50 tons of relief supplies to Colombia after a volcano erupts.

6 December: SAC completes equipping its first fully operational KC–10 Extender squadron with 19 aircraft at Barksdale AFB, Louisiana.

12 December: MAC C–130 Hercules and C–141 Starlifters perform 26 airlift missions to transport the remains of paratroopers of the 101st Airborne Division killed in an early morning crash of an Arrow Air DC–8 at Gander, Newfoundland.

18 December: The Western Pacific Rescue Coordination Center coordinates a mission that rescues 78 people from the sinking ship, *Asunción Cinco,* near Lubang, Republic of the Philippines.

1986

8 January: MAC accepts delivery of its first C–5B Galaxy at Altus AFB, Oklahoma.

8 January: The first overseas meteorological data system circuit is accepted at Eielson AFB, Alaska. This event marks the initial milestone in the replacement of obsolete weather teletype systems with more modern equipment in Alaska, Europe, and the Pacific.

28 January: The space shuttle *Challenger* and its seven-person crew are lost in an explosion shortly after lift-off from John F. Kennedy Space Center. NASA suspends the U.S.–manned space program until the cause can be identified and corrected.

18–22 February: The 129th Aerospace Rescue and Recovery Group and the 41st ARRS employ four H–3 Jolly Green Giant helicopters, two HH–53 helicopters, and three C–130 Hercules aircraft to assist flood victims of the Russian River and Yuba River valleys of northern California. The airmen rescue 33 flood victims and supply over 3,000 sandbags to Army troops responding to the disaster site.

25–26 February: Following a disputed election in the Republic of the Philippines, the 31st ARRS flies five H–3 Jolly Green Giant helicopters to the presidential palace in Manila and evacuates President Ferdinand Marcos and 51 other persons from the palace to Clark AB. Subsequently, U.S. aircraft fly Marcos and his family to Andersen AFB and then to Hickam AFB.

3 March: TAC's first OT–38 Talon replaces the Cessna O–2 aircraft at Shaw AFB, South Carolina.

4 March: USAF approves SAC's concept for refueling foreign aircraft participating in joint exercises. Under this policy, SAC tankers refuel the first foreign aircraft, an Egyptian model, during Exercise Bright Star, a joint U.S.–Egyptian operation.

5 March: Responding to the McCollum Amendment of 1986 authorizing humanitarian aid to refugees, USAF begins airlifting Afghan patients and refugees from Pakistan to the United States.

5 March: Capt Marc C. Felman and his KC–10 Extender crew perform an emergency refueling in mid-Atlantic of Marine A–4M aircraft during a Coronet East deployment, an action for which they will receive the Mackay Trophy for the most meritorious flight of 1986.

25 March: For the first time, an all-woman crew, assigned to the 351st Strategic Missile Wing, Whiteman AFB, Missouri, stands Minuteman missile alert.

5–6 April: Four C–141 Starlifters and one H–3 Jolly Green Giant helicopter of the 63d Military Airlift Wing transport large amounts of fire-suppressant foam and airlifts burn victims from Osan AB after the explosion of a 700,000-gallon tank of jet fuel. Burn victims are helicoptered from Osan to Seoul for medical treatment.

14–15 April: The U.S. forces launch Operation Eldorado Canyon, a retaliatory bombing raid in response to terrorist activities supported by Libyan leader Muammar Qadhafi. Twenty-eight KC–10 Extenders and KC–135 Stratotankers depart the RAF bases at Fairford and Mildenhall, England, followed shortly by 24 F–111 Ravens from the British base at Lakenheath, England. As the F–111 strike force is bombing its Libyan targets, KC–10s refuel it six times, in complete radio silence, before returning to England.

15 April: One of five rocket bombs launched from an off-base location lands inside the perimeter of Yokota AB. It causes minor property damage but does not injure any base personnel.

18 April: A Titan 34D space booster explodes shortly after lift-off from Space Launch Complex Four at Vandenberg

AFB. The launch complex is closed for repairs until 15 August.

28 April–7 May: Air Weather Service units support the efforts of the United States to track the movement of radioactive contamination from the Chernobyl reactor accident in the USSR. The service provides extensive data and modeling, as well as air-sampling missions by WC–130 Hercules aircraft.

19 June: All USAF Rapier surface-to-air missile units in Europe become operationally ready.

19–28 July: Twenty-four C–141 Starlifters and eight C–130 Hercules aircraft fly 32 missions during Operation Southern Haylift, supplying 535.9 tons of donated hay (more than 19,000 bales) to drought-stricken farmers in seven southeastern states. The operation helps save hundreds of cattle and with them the livelihoods of a great many southern livestock farmers.

27 July: A C–9 Nightingale flies Father Lawrence Jenco, who was released as a hostage by Muslim extremists in Lebanon, from Damascus to USAFE Medical Center at Rhein-Main AB.

27–29 August: A C–130 Hercules from the 50th Tactical Airlift Squadron airlifts 250 tents to villagers of northwestern Cameroon, West Africa, when a cloud of carbon dioxide bubbles up from the depths of Lake Nyos. Over 2,000 inhabitants of this volcanic region seek refuge at villages located away from the lake.

1 September: The last Cessna O–2 aircraft of the TAC is sent to storage at Davis-Monthan AFB.

5 September: A USAFE C–141 Starlifter flies Americans injured in a hijacking attempt at Karachi Airport, Pakistan, to Frankfurt, Germany, for medical attention at U.S. military hospitals.

18–20 September: Two C–5 Galaxies of the 436th Military Airlift Wing transport 93 tons of medical supplies and food to Luzon, Republic of the Philippines, under the terms of the Denton Amendment to the Foreign Assistance Act of 1985.

While in the United States, President Aquino personally accepts the gifts of medicine and food.

11–16 October: USAF airlifts medicine and other relief supplies to El Salvador's capital city after a devastating earthquake destroys 96 percent of its structures.

7 December: A WC–130 Hercules aircraft transports seven tons of food, clothing, candles, and other emergency supplies to Saipan, Mariana Islands, after Typhoon Kim devastates the island. The 54th Weather Reconnaissance Squadron piggybacked their traditional Christmas "gift drop" for Saipan's children with the relief supplies.

10 December: A HC–130 Hercules, along with a UH–60 Black Hawk, a CH–3 Jolly Green Giant, and an MH–53 helicopter, rescue 19 survivors aboard the Norwegian ship *Geco Alpha*, a 300-foot seismograph research vessel that has caught fire about 30 miles from Destin, Florida. Survivors are transported to Eglin AFB for medical evaluation and treatment.

18–20 December: Two H–3 Jolly Green Giant helicopters from the 31st ARRS rescue 13 survivors of the Philippine inter-island ship, the *Asunción* Cinco, from the South China Sea, about 95 miles southwest of Manila. Those rescued receive medical treatment at Cubi Point AS, Republic of the Philippines, for medical treatment.

22 December: The Peacekeeper ICBMs deployed in modified Minuteman silos achieve initial operational capability when the tenth Peacekeeper is placed on alert at Warren AFB.

CHRONOLOGY
1987-1997

1987

16 January: A B–1B Lancer from Edwards AFB launches the first short-range attack missile from a B–1B bomber over the Tonopah Test Range, Nevada.

13–15 February: Two C–141 Starlifters and two C–130 Hercules cargo aircraft move 64 tons of tents and plastic sheeting to Vanuatu, New Hebrides, after Typhoon Uma strikes its central islands. In addition, U.S. humanitarian aircraft search the area around Vanuata for shipwrecked survivors.

16 February: The Joint Military Medical Command activates at San Antonio, Texas, and is staffed by both Air Force and Army personnel.

5 May: SAC removes the last active Titan II missile from alert duty at Little Rock AFB, Arkansas, ending the operational life of the nation's largest ICBM.

6 May: The 43d Electronics Combat Squadron, 66th Elec-tronic Combat Wing, from Sembach AB takes possession of its first EC–130H Compass Call aircraft.

4 July–17 September: Detachment 15 of the Air Force Plant Representative Office and the B–1B Special Project Office establish world and national speed, distance, and payload records in B–1B aircraft. They will receive the Mackay Trophy for their achievements.

17 July: Air Force Logistics Command (AFLC) rolls out the first enhanced MH–53J helicopter equipped with Pave Low III, a night and adverse weather navigational system, at Pensacola Naval AS, Florida.

22 July–21 December: The Air Force provides tanker support to Navy fighter aircraft during Operation Earnest Will over the Persian Gulf. The naval aircraft protect Kuwaiti convoys from Iranian attack during the war between Iran and Iraq.

31 August–9 September: Eight C–130 Hercules and a large number of C–141 Starlifters fly 2,511 tons of fire retardant and a contingent of fire fighters to the coastal areas of Oregon and California to combat forest fires blazing across 970 square miles of forest, brush, and scrub land.

24 September: The first-ever Thunderbirds show in Beijing, China, attracts an audience in excess of 20,000.

1 October: PACAF retires its last seven T–33 two-seater training aircraft at Hickam AFB and the same number at Clark AB ending 32 years of T-Bird operations in the command.

November–December: MAC transports federal marshals and sharpshooters to suppress Cuban detainee rioting at several U.S. federal correction centers.

24 November: A B–1B Lancer bomber records the first success of an air-launched cruise missile.

5 December: Six C–130 Hercules aircraft of the 374th Tactical Airlift Wing move more than 34 tons of relief supplies, including clothing and rice, to victims of Typhoon Nina on the island of Luzon, Republic of the Philippines. The wing also incorporates its annual toy "Christmas drop" for the storm victims' children with the relief supplies.

8 December: The United States and the USSR sign the Intermediate–Range Nuclear Forces (INF) Treaty. The treaty pledges the two nations to remove Pershing II, GLCMs, and SS–20 intermediate-range (620–3,415 statute miles) missiles from Europe. The agreement will result in the inactivation of six GLCM wings in Europe: the 303d TMW, RAF Molesworth, United Kingdom; the 38th TMW, Wuescheim AS, Germany; the 487th TMW, Comiso AS, Italy; the 485th TMW, Florennes AB; the 486th TMW, Woensdrecht AB, the Netherlands; and the 501st TMW, RAF Greenham Common, United Kingdom.

1988

1 January: SAC changes Minuteman and Peacekeeper ICBM crew assignment policy to permit mixed male/female crews in Minuteman and Peacekeeper missile launch facilities. Heretofore, SAC has segregated male and female crews.

20 January: The 100th and final B–1B Lancer bomber rolls off the assembly line at Rockwell's aircraft plant in Palmdale, California.

25–28 January: At the request of the Philippine government, Manila receives 102 tons of medical supplies via two C–5 Galaxy transports of the 60th Military Airlift Wing. The supplies are donated by a private relief organization, Americares, to replenish the Philippine stock.

19–22 February: A C–141 Starlifter of the 86th Military Airlift Squadron, 60th Military Airlift Wing, transports 50 tons of construction materials and electrical equipment to the Marshall Islands to repair housing and restore electrical power damage caused by Typhoon Roy.

17–18 March: USAF transport aircraft carry some 3,200 U.S. soldiers to the Republic of Honduras to support Exercise Golden Pheasant. The deployment is requested by the Honduran government after Sandinista forces from Nicaragua invade their country.

April: SAC tankers give extensive refueling support to U.S. Navy aircraft attacking Iranian warships and offshore oil platforms in the Persian Gulf.

April: Eight C–5 Galaxies and 22 C–141 Starlifters of MAC transport 1,300 security specialists from the United States to the Republic of Panama to counteract the political instability that threatens the safety of several thousand U.S. citizens.

17 April–23 July: Capt Michael Eastman and his C–5 Galaxy transport crew are the first U.S. airmen to land at Semipalatinsk, Republic of Kazakhstan, USSR. They deliver sensitive verification equipment for monitoring nuclear tests under existing international agreements. Captain Eastman receives the Mackay Trophy for successful execution of this mission.

May: The 60th Military Airlift Wing transports 73 tons of relief supplies by a C–5 Galaxy from Kadena AB to Islamabad, Pakistan, to refugees fleeing the civil war in nearby Afghanistan. USAF aircraft also fly Afghans requiring medical attention from Pakistan to hospitals in Europe or the United States.

2 June and 10–11 August: Fighting between rebels and government forces in southern Sudan drives hundreds of thousands of people seeking food and shelter to refugee

A KC–135 tanker refuels an F–117 Stealth fighter. Designers incorporated radical design and radar-absorbing materials to enable the aircraft to evade radar detection.

camps. At the request of the Sudanese government, the 60th and 436th Military Airlift Wings fly humanitarian missions. These units furnish more than 70 tons of plastic sheeting for shelters, in addition to food and other supplies.

August: USAF MAC C–5 Galaxies airlift a 500-member United Nations peacekeeping force from the United States to Turkey and Iraq to monitor a cease-fire agreement between these two countries.

1 August: The 177th Fighter Group retires the last three F–106 Delta Darts from the active USAF inventory of on-line aircraft. Two of the F–106s are "A" models and one is a "B" model.

22 August–6 October: Thirteen separate fires burn in more than half of Yellowstone National Park's 2.2 million acres over portions of Wyoming and Montana. Active and Reserve MAC aircraft transport more than 4,000 firefighters and nearly 2,500 tons of fire-fighting equipment to the scene of the disaster. Aircraft are fitted with Forest Service modular airborne fire-fighting equipment that sprays fire retardant chemicals at low altitudes.

25–31 August: A civil war in Somalia results in large-scale requirements for medical treatment of people fleeing to

Mogadishu, the capital. The Somali government requests medical aid, particularly hospital beds. A C–141 Starlifter of the 41st Military Airlift Squadron responds with a 200-bed emergency hospital weighing more than 22 tons.

28 August–3 September: As a result of shortages of hospital equipment and medical supplies on the island of Sao Tome off the west coast of Africa, a C–141 Starlifter of the 20th Military Airlift Squadron flies 29 tons of supply items to that location.

September: USAF E–3A Sentry AWACS aircraft and fighter escorts fly sorties over the South Korean Olympic Games in Seoul to deter North Korean aggression.

10–15 September: The 60th, 62d, 63d, and 436th Military Airlift Wings fly at least 100 tons of relief supplies and a field hospital to the victims of a flood in Bangladesh. The flood inundates three-fourths of the country and almost all of the capital city of Dhaka, killing 1,200 people and making 28 million inhabitants homeless.

29 September: The long stand-down of the U.S. manned space program in the wake of the *Challenger* tragedy of 28 January 1986 ends with the launch of the space shuttle *Discovery*.

25 October: The 31st ARRS uses two HH–3 Jolly Green Giant helicopters to rescue 27 stranded residents following a flood caused by Typhoon Ruby at Marikina, Republic of the Philippines, near Manila. The four-flight mission takes eight airborne hours to accomplish this effort.

9 November: In response to a State Department request, a C–5 Galaxy of the 709th Military Airlift Squadron transports a mobile dental clinic and two ambulances to Niamey, Niger, on a humanitarian mission.

10 November: USAF reveals the F–117A Stealth fighter to the public for the first time. Manufactured by Lockheed, using radar-absorbent materials and a radical new design, the F–117A can evade radar detection.

16–30 November: After a destructive influx of locusts, the 60th, 63d, 437th, and 438th Military Airlift Wings fly 442 tons of insecticide and supplies on a humanitarian mission to Dakar, Senegal.

22 November: USAF, in partnership with the Northrop Aviation Corporation, rolls out the first B–2 Stealth bomber in Palmdale, California. Like the F–117A, the B–2 has an extremely small radar signature.

Late November: Civil strife, natural disasters, and territorial threats result in humanitarian airlifts by the 9th Military Airlift Squadron of an ambulance to Douala, capital of Cameroon, and 31 pallets of medical equipment to N'Djamena, capital of Chad—70 tons in all for both countries.

9 December: The United States offers disaster relief to the Soviet government, which Mikhail Gorbachev accepts. Over an eight-week period, MAC units transport more than 311 tons of relief cargo to victims of an earthquake in Yerevan, Armenia, the USSR. This operation sets a precedent because previously the USSR had prohibited direct U.S. flights to its cities without Soviet personnel aboard as observers.

12 December: The 33d ARRS saves 11 passengers afloat in a life raft from the sunken ship, *Selina*, in the Pacific Ocean between the Philippines and Japan. The survivors receive transport to Clark AB for examination and treatment.

Late December: A C–141 Starlifter of the Twenty-first Air Force flies from the eastern United States to Nairobi, Kenya, carrying six tons of parachutes to be used as tents by homeless refugees in southern Sudan.

1989

7–20 January: Two C–130 Hercules of the 167th Tactical Airlift Group fly U.S. medical personnel and supplies to Liberia in support of Medfly '89, a joint-service humanitarian effort to train medical personnel, inoculate Liberians against disease, and treat their ailments.

Early February: Two C–141 Starlifters of the 63d Military Airlift Wing provide 20 tons of insecticide to Dakar, Senegal, to combat locust swarms.

16 February: Northrop completes the 3,806th T–38 Talon and closes the production line for this versatile jet trainer.

27 March: MAC assists oil cleanup efforts near Valdez, Alaska, after an oil tanker runs aground. MAC aircraft transport oil-spill cleanup equipment, cargo items, and personnel to the Valdez area.

April: A C–5 Galaxy of the 436th Military Airlift Wing transports 32 pallets of relief supplies to Banjul, Gambia; Malabo, Equatorial Guinea; and N'Djamena, Chad, as an act of humanitarian relief for the destitute population.

17 April: Lockheed delivers the 50th and last C–5B Galaxy transport to the U.S. Air Force.

9–11 June: MAC units fly four tons of medical supplies and a U.S. burn specialist to alleviate the suffering of victims of a rail disaster at Ufa on the Trans–Siberian Railroad about 750 miles southeast of Moscow. As a pair of trains carrying some 1,200 passengers pass each other, a liquid-gas pipeline explodes and causes one of the trains to derail and crash into the other. Approximately 850 passengers are either killed or injured, making it the worst rail disaster in history.

A C–130 Hercules flies low over Panama during Operation Just Cause in 1989.

10 June: Capt Jacquelyn S. Parker becomes the first woman pilot to graduate from the Air Force Test Pilot School at Edwards AFB.

14 June: The first successful launch of the Martin Marietta Titan IV heavy-lift space booster, nearly 20 stories tall, occurs at Cape Canaveral. It carries a classified military payload.

6 July: President Bush presents the Presidential Medal of Freedom, the nation's highest civilian award, to Gen James H. Doolittle, USAF, retired, at the White House. General Doolittle led the famous World War II raid on Tokyo.

Late July–7 August: A raging fire spreads through thousands of acres of forest in southwestern Idaho near Boise, in eastern Oregon, and in eastern California near Van Nuys. MAC aircraft transport nearly 1,000 firefighters and 850 tons of fire-fighting equipment and medical supplies to the scene. Other USAF aircraft spray 3,350 tons of chemical fire retardant on the conflagration from low altitude.

16–25 August: PACAF hosts the first Pacific Air Chiefs Conference attended by representatives from Australia, Japan, the Philippines, Singapore, Malaysia, and Brunei. The conference promotes regional cooperation and security by enhancing each nation's air power.

19 September: One hundred twenty-eight aircraft of MAC and the Eighth Air Force provide relief to victims of Hurricane Hugo. Winds of 125 mph along with torrential rains and high seas destroy the homes of tens of thousands of inhabitants of the Lesser Antilles and South Carolina. A critical absence or shortage of food, water, and electricity brings about the transportation of some 2,000 people and 4,330 tons of supplies.

1 October: Gen Hansford T. Johnson, USAF, becomes the first Air Force Academy graduate to become a four-star general.

3 October: USAF receives the last of 37 Lockheed U–2R high-altitude reconnaissance aircraft.

4 October: The B–1B crew of the 96th Bombardment Wing at Dyess AFB receives the Mackay Trophy for successfully landing their aircraft with a retracted-nose landing gear. This accomplishment is the first-ever gear-up landing of a B–1. No aircrew were injured and the airplane suffered only minimal damages.

4 October: A C–5B Galaxy lands without skis at McMurdo Station in Antarctica with 72 passengers and 84 tons of cargo, including two fully assembled Bell UH–IN helicopters. This is the first time an aircraft so large has landed on the ice continent. The crew of the 60th Military Airlift Wing at Travis AFB carries out the mission.

17 October: Units of MAC respond to a devastating earthquake measuring 7.1 on the Richter scale in the San Francisco Bay, California, area. They deliver more than 250 tons of relief equipment and transport some 100 passengers.

14 December: For the first time, MAC allows women to serve as crew members on C–130 and C–141 airdrop missions. This marks the entry of women into combat crew roles.

20 December: Operation Just Cause witnesses the use of the Lockheed F–117A Stealth fighter-bomber in combat operations for the first time. Two Stealth fighters of the 37th Tactical Fighter Wing release their 2,000-pound laser-guided bombs in the vicinity of the Panama Defense Forces's barracks located on the Rio Hato military reservation.

20 December: An AC–130H aircrew of the Air Force Special Operations Command accurately attacks the Panamanian Defense Forces headquarters compound, the most heavily defended target of the Just Cause operation. Subsequently, U.S. forces are able to occupy key strategic military positions in Panama.

20 December: In Operation Just Cause, MAC units transport 9,500 airborne troops from Pope AFB to Panama in less than 36 hours, making it the largest night-combat airdrop since the Normandy invasion of 1944.

20–31 December: AFRES crews make a major contribution to the success of Just Cause, flying 455 sorties totaling 1,500 hours. Reserve airlifters carry more than 5,900 passengers and 3,700 tons of cargo. Air refuelers support regular and reserve aircraft. Reservists fly AC–130 gunships on 29 sorties and expend over 7,000 rounds of ammunition.

20–31 December: Numerous ANG fighter, special operations, and airlift units participate in Operation Just Cause. They are the 114th and 180th Tactical Fighter Groups, the 193d Special Operations Group, and the 105th, 136th, 139th, 146th, 166th, and 172d Tactical Airlift Groups.

29–31 December: Two C–130 Hercules of the 435th Tactical Airlift Wing and the 37th Tactical Airlift Squadron transport 31 tons of medical supplies to Bucharest, Romania, for treatment of civilians wounded in a violent anticommunist revolution. The fighting subsides with the victory of the anticommunist rebels and the subsequent execution of President Nicolas Ceaucescu.

1990

31 January: After more than 11 years, the ANG's rotational deployments to defend the Panama Canal, known as Operation Coronet Cove closes. The ANG flew more than 13,000 sorties, totaling 16,959 hours, since the operation began in 1979.

February: Units of the 436th Military Airlift Wing and the 463d Tactical Airlift Wing make flights to Monrovia, Liberia, providing assistance for hundreds of people displaced by a civil war. The airlifters transport 30 tons of relief supplies.

February–March: Aircraft of the 60th and 63d Military Airlift Wings deliver 410 tons of relief supplies and 149 construction workers from nearby islands to Western and American Samoa to assist residents' recovery from the ravages of Typhoon Ofa.

23 February–6 March: Units of the 435th Tactical Airlift Wing fly 11 tons of medical equipment and relief supplies, as well as 60 medics, to treat disease and provide inoculations against infection in Senegal.

4 April: The U.S. Air Force adds to its inventory the last of 60 official KC–10A Extender tanker/cargo aircraft built by McDonnell Douglas.

11 April: A C–5 Galaxy transports to the United States the first European-based GLCM scheduled for destruction in accordance with the INF Treaty.

June: Secretary of the Air Force Donald B. Rice releases *Global Reach—Global Power,* a transitional strategic planning framework for the Air Force following the Cold War.

Late June–Early July: The Painted Cave fire begins in the forest north of Santa Barbara, California. It eventually burns 4,900 acres and destroys 450 homes. At least ten C–130 Hercules, flown by crews from MAC units, deliver fire-suppressant chemicals, fire fighters, and fire-fighting equipment to the disaster area. The aircraft also sprays the fire from the air.

12 July: The U.S. Air Force accepts delivery of the last of 59 Lockheed F–117A Stealth fighter-bombers.

17 July–1 August: An earthquake measuring 7.7 on the Richter scale strikes Baguio, in the Philippines, only 45 miles from Clark AB. The 60th, 62d, and 438th Military Airlift Wings, as well as the 374th Tactical Airlift Wing, deliver 582 tons of relief supplies and transport 2,475 passengers to the disaster area to assist the injured and the homeless.

24 July: Following the end of the Cold War, nearly 30 years of continuous airborne command-post operations and over 250 million hours of accident-free flying cease when the SAC commander in chief's EC–135C Looking Glass lands. Looking Glass aircraft are airborne nuclear command and control posts.

August–December: Air Force Space Command (AFSPACECOM) establishes the first space system infrastructure to directly support a military conflict. Created to assist allied forces in the Persian Gulf region, the space satellite systems will relay communications, facilitate navigation, provide meteorological data, and detect short-range ballistic missile launches.

7 August: Operation Desert Shield begins in response to Iraq's 2 August invasion of Kuwait and the ensuing threat to Saudi Arabian security. The operation's immediate objective is to protect Saudi Arabia from Iraqi aggression and build up allied military strength for the liberation of Kuwait should diplomacy fail to dislodge the Iraqi army.

7 August: In response to the Iraqi invasion of Kuwait, 24 F–15C Eagles of the TAC's 71st Tactical Fighter Squadron make a 15-hour, 8,000-mile nonstop flight from Langley AFB to Dhahran, Saudi Arabia, with 12 in-flight refuelings.

8 August: The first USAF transport, a C–141 Starlifter, to fly into the Gulf crisis zone lands in Dhahran. The crew are the first USAF reservists to arrive in Saudi Arabia.

9 August: The Alaskan Air Command is redesignated as the Eleventh Air Force and assigned to PACAF.

17 August: President Bush activates the Civil Reserve Air Fleet for the first time since it was authorized in 1952. The activation increases airlift availability for the Middle East.

20 August: More than 15,300 USAF reservists, approximately 22 percent of the total USAF Reserve force, volunteer to serve in Operation Desert Shield.

22 August: By this date, Reserve volunteers of Operation Desert Shield log more than 4,300 flying hours, transport 7 million tons of cargo, and provide travel for 8,150 persons.

23 August: The 89th Military Airlift Wing receives the first of two Boeing VC–25A presidential transport aircraft at Andrews AFB. The VC–25A is a modified 747–200B commercial transport that replaces the VC–137C Air Force One.

23 August: Secretary of Defense Richard B. Cheney grants the Air Force authority to call up reservists for active duty in the Gulf crisis. Eventually the USAF calls more than 20,000 Air Force reservists to active duty.

29 August: An Air Force C–5 Galaxy of the 68th Military Airlift Squadron, carrying medical and other supplies destined for the Gulf theater, crashes on take-off from Ramstein AB. Thirteen persons are killed and four injured. SSgt Lorenzo Galvin Jr., a reservist, is awarded the Airman's Medal for his heroic efforts to rescue victims of the crash.

6 September: The United States Postal Service honors Lt Gen Claire L. Chennault, organizer of the famous World War II Flying Tigers, by issuing a 40-cent stamp that features his portrait.

8 September: Marcelite Jordan Harris becomes the first black woman to hold the grade of brigadier general in the U.S. Air Force. A specialist in aircraft maintenance, General Harris becomes Air Training Command's director of technical training.

17 September: Secretary Cheney removes Gen Michael J. Dugan as Air Force chief of staff for unauthorized comments to the media in Saudi Arabia during Operation Desert Shield.

18–28 September: The 436th and 438th Military Airlift Wings transport 107 pallets of tents, cots, and blankets, as well as 360 passengers, to Jordan for the relief of some 100,000 foreign workers from Kuwait. More than 600,000 individuals eventually flee to Jordan after the invasion by Iraq.

1–2 December: Two MH–60 Pave Hawk helicopters of the 38th Air Rescue Squadron at Osan AB rescue 22 shipwrecked sailors from a grounded Panamanian vessel located approximately six miles west of Kunsan AB.

29 December: The 169th Tactical Fighter Group is the first ANG unit to deploy to the Persian Gulf region for Operation Desert Shield.

1991

1991: Air Force Chief of Staff Gen Merrill A. McPeak designates the year 1991 as the "Year of Organization." Restructuring the Air Force to accommodate post–Cold War force reductions, he decreases the number of units,

A USAF F–16 Fighting Falcon rolls into the sun in the Arabian desert during Operation Desert Storm. The aircraft became operational in 1981.

eliminates divisions, and introduces the "one base, one wing, one boss" concept.

17 January: The Gulf War begins at 0300 hours with coalition air attacks against Iraqi targets; Operation Desert Shield becomes Operation Desert Storm. During the first 14 hours of the new operation, coalition aircraft fly more than 1,200 combat sorties against targets in Iraq and Kuwait.

17 January: B–52G Stratofortress crews from the 2d Bomb Wing of the Eighth Air Force, SAC, fly from Barksdale AFB to the Iraqi combat zone, launch 35 cruise missiles against targets in Iraq, and return to Barksdale. This event marks the longest bombing mission in history.

17 January: Constituting less than 2.5 percent of all coalition aircraft, F-117A Stealth fighter-bomber crews attack more than 31 percent of Iraqi strategic targets during the first day of the Gulf War.

17 January: C–130s begin airlifting elements of the Army XVIII Airborne Corps from eastern Saudi Arabia to Rafha, on the Saudi-Iraqi border. Flying more than 300 sorties a

131

day in ten-minute intervals, the C–130s deliver 13,843 troops and 9,396 tons of cargo. This movement enables coalition forces to encircle Iraq's Republican Guard in what Gen Norman Schwarzkopf, commander in chief, US Central Command, describes as the "Hail Mary maneuver."

17 January–28 February: In 42 days of combat, 16 C–130 Hercules aircraft of the AFRES 1650th Tactical Airlift Wing (Provisional) fly more than 3,200 combat sorties against Iraq. A–10 Thunderbolt IIs of the Reserve 706th Tactical Fighter Squadron fly more than 1,000 combat sorties against enemy targets. Even though some aircraft sustain combat damage, no Reserve aircraft is lost and no reservist is killed in combat operations during the Gulf War.

18 January: USAF aircraft based at Incirlik, Turkey, begin flying strike missions against targets in northern Iraq to prevent reinforcement of enemy forces in Kuwait.

21 January: Capt Paul T. Johnson in his A–10 Thunderbolt II aircraft locates a U.S. Navy fighter pilot who had ejected

B–52G Stratofortresses flew the longest bombing mission in history—over 35 hours—in Operation Desert Storm, round-trip from Barksdale AFB, Louisiana, to Iraq.

in Iraqi territory and destroys a threatening Iraqi truck. This action allows an Air Force MH–53J Pave Low helicopter to rescue the pilot. Captain Johnson will be awarded the Air Force Cross; the Pave Low helicopter crew will receive the Mackay Trophy for their heroism.

22–23 January: F–111F Aardvarks use laser-guided "smart bombs" against hardened aircraft shelters at Al Asad AB, Iraq.

27 January: Two F–111F Aardvarks deliver precision bombs on the refinery at Al Ahmadi, Kuwait, which closes oil manifolds opened by Iraqi forces. Their attack stops the flow of crude oil into the Persian Gulf.

27 January: Coalition aircraft attain air supremacy in the Gulf War after ten days of aerial combat.

6 February: Reserve Capt Robert R. Swain of the 706th Tactical Fighter Squadron scores the first-ever A–10 Warthog air-to-air kill by shooting down an Iraqi helicopter.

13 February: F–117 Stealth fighter-bombers bomb a communications center, the Al Firdas bunker, in downtown Baghdad, unaware of its function as a civilian shelter. Several hundred civilians are casualties. As a consequence, coalition air authorities control combat missions in the capital city more tightly.

21 February: At the request of the U.S. State Department, a C–141 Starlifter of the 438th Military Airlift Wing flies 55 tons of relief supplies to Freetown, Sierra Leone, to alleviate economic hardship.

24 February: Ground offensive against Iraq begins. Within 100 hours, coalition ground forces, coupled with continued air attacks, totally overwhelm the Iraqi ground troops. Between 24 and 28 February, USAF flies 3,000 combat (reconnaissance, close air support, interdiction) sorties.

25 February: USAF F–16 Fighting Falcons attack Iraqi forces surrounding a nine-man Army Special Forces team. The attack permits Army UH–60 Black Hawk helicopters to rescue the team.

28 February: The Gulf War ends at 0800 hours with a coalition-declared cease-fire. Overall, during the entire Gulf air war, the F–117A Stealth fighter-bombers have flown only 2 percent of the combat sorties but have attacked 40 percent of Iraqi strategic targets with the use of laser-guided bombs. Stealth aircraft made 1,270 combat sorties and dropped 2,041 tons of bombs with 79 percent or 1,616 tons of bombs hitting their targets. Coalition forces released approximately 16,000 precision-guided munitions against Iraqi forces and dropped some 210,000 unguided bombs. In 42 days of around-the-clock operations, USAF flew 59 percent of the nearly 110,000 combat sorties. U.S. aerial strength of approximately 1,990 aircraft comprised 75 percent of total coalition air power.

28 February: During the execution of Desert Shield/Desert Storm, AFSPACECOM's satellite systems relay 85 percent of the theater's communications; provide meteorological data critical to weapon selection and attack plans; detect all short-range ballistic missile launches and relayed data to Army antimissile batteries; and assist the navigation of ground forces maneuvering in desert terrain.

March: MAC C–5 Galaxies transport relief supplies to Kuwait following the seven-month occupation and destruction by Iraqi forces.

March–July: Forty-two C–5 Galaxies and three C–141 Starlifters of the 60th and 436th Military Airlift Wings transport more than 1,000 tons of fire-fighting equipment and some 100 firefighters to the Kuwait City area to extinguish more than 500 oil well fires set by the retreating Iraqi forces.

1 March–31 December: MAC C–5s transport 150 tons of relief supplies to Bucharest, Romania, to assist the government in overcoming a critical economic situation and restoring stability in the face of violent street demonstrations.

8 March: The first Martin Marietta Titan IV propelled by a heavy-lift space booster is launched from Vandenberg AFB. Augmenting the space shuttle, the Titan IV has two upper-stage options that enable it to carry several critical military payloads.

Early April: Two 436th Military Airlift Wing C–5 Galaxies carry 200 tons of medical supplies to Lima, Peru, after the

C–130 Hercules aircraft lifted airborne troops and cargo at the rate of 300 sorties per day during encircling maneuvers in Desert Storm.

outbreak of a cholera epidemic that afflicted nearly 150,000 people and killed more than 1,000.

5 April–15 July: More than a million Kurds flee Iraq under pressure from Saddam Hussein's forces. To alleviate the Kurdish distress, MAC units fly 7,000 tons of relief supplies to northern Iraq, southeastern Turkey, and western Iran.

12 April: F–15 Eagle alert crews from a forward operating base at Galena Airport, Alaska, make their first interception of a Soviet AN–74 Coaler aircraft.

18 April: USAF completes the first successful flight test of the Martin Marietta/Boeing ICBM (small version). The flight trajectory was 4,000 miles from Vandenberg AFB to the Pacific Island target area at the Kwajalein Missile Range.

10 May–13 June: A tropical cyclone bearing winds of 150 mph strikes the coast of Bangladesh and creates 20-foot tidal waves. Units of the Military Airlift Command and Special Operations transport more than 3,000 tons of relief supplies (including helicopters) and 510 passengers to Dhaka, Bangladesh.

31 May: Complying with the terms of the 1987 INF Treaty, the USAF inactivates the 501st TMW at RAF Greenham Common, United Kingdom. This wing, the first GLCM wing to activate in Europe and the first to become operational, is the last to inactivate.

June–September: In response to the extended drought in Ethiopia, at least 19 humanitarian missions by MAC organizations to Addis Ababa provide more than 1,000 tons of food, farm equipment, and medical supplies.

8 June–2 July: The eruption, more than 100,000 feet high, of Mount Pinatubo on the island of Luzon, the Philippines, covers Clark AB and two other U.S. military bases with two feet of volcanic ash. USAF evacuates more than 15,000 military personnel and civilian workers and their families, and provides during Operation Fiery Vigil more than 2,000 tons of humanitarian cargo for the thousands of Filipinos who are homeless, require medical attention, and lack food and clothing.

25 June: Due to drought-induced food shortages in Kenya, the 60th Military Airlift Wing delivers 80 tons of food rations to Nairobi.

July–August: MAC units transport 170 tons of food to Tirana, Albania, to offset shortages when the communist government collapses at the end of the Cold War. This is the first time since 1946 that the Albanian government allows U.S. personnel into the country.

7 July: After a drought and the accompanying food shortage aggravated by civil war, the 436th Military Airlift Wing delivers a 70-ton cargo of food and miscellaneous relief supplies to N'Djamena, Chad.

22 July: The 730th Military Airlift Squadron of the 445th Military Airlift Wing delivers nearly 20 tons of medical supplies to Ulan Bator, Mongolia, to overcome critical shortages. This is the first humanitarian mission flown to Mongolia by the U.S. Air Force.

6–9 August: MAC units transport 75 tons of blankets and medical supplies to Shanghai, China, where floods in central and eastern China have caused more than 1,000 fatalities and have left hundreds of thousands homeless.

22 August: USAF charters the Gulf War air power survey (GWAPS) to assess the role of air power in the Gulf War. The GWAPS is modeled after the post–World War II U.S. strategic bombing survey in form and style.

15 September: A C–17A Globemaster III transport makes its first flight from Long Beach, California, to the Air Force Flight Test Center at Edwards AFB. Capable of delivering outsized cargo in a tactical environment, the Globemaster III can operate from the same small, austere airfields as does the C–130 Hercules transport.

15 September: The first prototype of the T–1 Jayhawk flies at Edwards AFB. Similar to the Beechjet 400A corporate transport, the Jayhawk is intended for specialized undergraduate pilot training.

27 September: President Bush orders termination of SAC's alert, initiated in October 1957. The next day the alert forces cease operations, heralding the successful conclusion of the Cold War.

27 September–3 October: A mutiny of soldiers joined by rebellious civilians in Kinshasa, Zaire, endangers the lives

Air Force C–5 cargo aircraft delivered many tons of relief supplies to Armenia after the collapse of the former Soviet Union.

of foreigners. The president of Zaire helps the foreigners escape. MAC units evacuate more than 1,000 persons.

October–November: Following 16 years of civil war and a deteriorating economy, Angola accepts humanitarian assistance from the United States. The 436th Military Airlift Wing carries 275 tons of relief supplies to Luanda.

2 October: Flying the USAF's second humanitarian mission to Mongolia, the 834th Airlift Division transports 15 pallets of medical supplies and eight ambulances to Ulan Bator. The collapse of the Soviet Union has severed Outer Mongolia from its traditional source of medical supplies.

23 October: Military airlift units transport 146 tons of medical supplies and relief cargo to Kiev, the Ukraine, to relieve stresses to the economy and the public health system associated with the collapse of the Soviet Union.

November: The MAC performs its 100th humanitarian mission. It is in relief of Afghan refugees fleeing to Pakistan. From early March 1986, MAC has transported 1,000 tons of relief cargo, utilizing C–5 Galaxies and C–141 Starlifters.

1 November: After the crash of a Canadian C–130 Hercules in Greenland, a Twenty-second Air Force C–5 Galaxy from Elmendorf AFB loaded with a 36-member search and rescue team from the Alaskan ANG, and two MH–60G Pave Hawk helicopters fly to Thule, Greenland. The American airmen locate the crash scene some 300 miles from the North Pole and rescue 13 survivors.

14 November: A C–5 Galaxy of the 436th Military Airlift Wing carries 50 tons of medical and relief supplies to Freetown, Sierra Leone, to alleviate the economic hardships and deprivations of the populace.

26 November: The lowering of the American flag at Clark AB signals the closing of the largest overseas U.S. Air Force base in the world as well as the end of more than 90 years of U.S. presence there.

6 December: Tropical Cyclone Zelda batters the Marshall Islands with high winds, heavy rain, and rough seas. The 834th Airlift Division responds with six C–130 Hercules aircraft loads of humanitarian supplies to the Kwajalein Atoll.

17–22 December: The 436th, 438th, and 439th Airlift Wings transport 238 tons of food and relief supplies to the former Soviet cities of Moscow and Saint Petersburg in Russia; Minsk in Byelorussia; and Yerevan in Armenia. These humanitarian missions seek to alleviate food shortages and other scarcities of everyday necessities resulting from the economic disintegration of the Soviet Union.

21 December: The Rockwell AC–130U Spectre gunship flies for the first time. The new-generation gunship combines increased firepower, reliability, and accuracy with the latest target-location technology.

1992

17 January: In a move to modernize its fleet of training aircraft, the Air Force accepts the first production model T–1A Jayhawk.

20–25 January: In response to a State Department request, a 60th Airlift Wing C–5 Galaxy airlifts 36 pallets of medical supplies weighing 56 tons from Japan to Mongolia, where health care resources are insufficient.

30 January: AFSPACECOM assumes control of Defense Department satellites and the operation and management of the Air Force Satellite Control Network.

6 February: Four C–130 Hercules aircraft of the 435th Tactical Airlift Wing transport food and medical supplies from American air bases in Germany to Lithuania, which in late 1991 had secured independence from the Soviet Union.

10–26 February: Provide Hope I, a humanitarian airlift operation, delivers thousands of tons of food and medical supplies to the Commonwealth of Independent States, former republics of the recently dissolved USSR. USAF flies 65 C–5 Galaxy and C–141 Starlifter missions in support of the operation.

29 February : Operation Provide Hope II begins. Like Provide Hope I, it transports American food and medical supplies to the former USSR. The U.S. Air Force flies in supplies, while the U.S. Navy and U.S. Army transport more cargo by sea and land.

4 March: Two B–52 Stratofortresses land in Russia on a friendship mission, demonstrating that the Cold War is over. This is the first landing by U.S. bombers in Russia since World War II.

15 March–18 April: USAF C–5 Galaxy and C–130 Hercules aircraft transport more than 165 tons of food, medical supplies, clothing, blankets, and other cargo to eastern Turkey for the relief of earthquake victims.

19 March: Two USAF F–15 Eagles intercept two Russian Tu–95 Bear bombers off the Alaskan coast—the first such sighting since the breakup of the Soviet Union.

24 March: The last USAF fighter aircraft to be stationed in Spain departs, ending a 26-year span of service in that country.

24 March: The U.S. joins 24 other nations in signing the Open Skies Treaty, which allows unarmed aerial reconnaissance flights over any signatory nation.

April: After an outbreak of oil fires, five USAF C–141 Starlifter aircraft deliver tons of fire-fighting equipment to Uzbekistan, a former Soviet republic.

1 April: A 437th Airlift Wing C–141 Starlifter drops 115 barrels of aviation fuel to a floating U.S.–Russian ice station in Antarctica to be used in its scientific research helicopters.

7 April: The United States recognizes the independence of Bosnia-Herzegovina, Croatia, and Slovenia, which declare independence from Serb-dominated Yugoslavia. Serb rebellions in Croatia and Bosnia-Herzegovina precipitate a protracted civil war.

18 April: USAF C–141 Starlifter cargo aircraft begin airlifting humanitarian relief supplies, such as food, medicine, and blankets, to Sarajevo, capital of the new republic of

Bosnia-Herzegovina, which is reeling from the collapse of the centralized economy.

24 April: Two Peruvian fighters attack and heavily damage an unarmed USAF C–130 Hercules aircraft flying in international airspace off Peru. For making a safe emergency landing, the C–130 crew will receive the Mackay Trophy.

1–11 May: After race riots erupt in Los Angeles, MAC aircraft transport troops, police, and their equipment to southern California.

3–4 May: Following a military coup in west Africa, a USAF C–141 Starlifter and a C–130 Hercules transport aircraft airlift 350 endangered foreign nationals, including Americans, from Sierra Leone.

7–8 May: The Command Band of the AFRES marches in a parade in Moscow, becoming the first U.S. military band to visit the Russian capital.

Mid-1992: The last EC–135 aircraft ceases Looking Glass operations.

1 June: In a major reorganization, the U.S. Air Force inactivates SAC, TAC, and MAC. It also activates Air Combat Command (ACC) and Air Mobility Command (AMC), comprising most of the resources of the inactivated commands.

1 June: DOD activates a new unified command, the United States Strategic Command, composed of Air Force and Navy elements. The last commander of SAC, Gen George L. Butler, becomes the first commander of the United States Strategic Command.

30 June: AMC completes the withdrawal of U.S. stockpiles overseas of nuclear artillery shells, Lance missile warheads, and naval depth charges in support of President George Bush's Nuclear Forces Initiative.

1 July: Continuing reorganization, the Air Force inactivates AFLC and AFSC, replacing them with the Air Force Materiel Command (AFMC).

3 July: The U.S. European Command launches Operation Provide Promise to provide regular relief flights to Bosnia-Herzegovina. Eventually USAF delivers tens of thousands of tons of food, medical supplies, and other humanitarian cargo to Sarajevo and other Bosnian communities, using C–130, C–141, C–5, and C–9 aircraft.

2–20 August: AMC transports U.S. forces to Kuwait in support of Operation Intrinsic Action, an exercise intended as a show of force to Iraq.

12 August–7 October: USAF C–130s fly missions in support of Operation Provide Transition in Angola. In preparation for Angola's first democratic elections, the aircraft transport demobilized soldiers to their homes after 16 years of civil war.

18 August: Operation Southern Watch, which forbids Iraqi flights south of 32 degrees north latitude, begins.

21 August–28 February 1993: After drought and civil war produce mass starvation in Somalia and forces thousands of people to enter refugee camps, USAF aircraft fly more than 3,000 missions transporting over 23,000 tons of food, water, medicine, and other relief supplies. This is called Operation Provide Relief.

25 August–28 October: After Hurricane Andrew hits southern Florida with sustained winds of 140 mph, humanitarian airlift flights transport 13,500 relief workers and more than 21,000 tons of relief supplies on 724 missions. Catastrophic hurricane damage forces Homestead AFB to close permanently.

31 August–Early September: A USAF C–141 airlifts 70 children suffering from cancer in the wake of the Chernobyl nuclear plant accident in the former USSR from Minsk, Byelorussia, to Brussels, Belgium, for specialized medical treatment.

1–25 September: After Typhoon Omar hits Guam with 150-mph winds and 16-inch rains, USAF transports 750 relief workers and almost 2,000 tons of supplies to the western Pacific island.

12 September–18 October: Following Typhoon Iniki, which devastates Kauai in the Hawaiian archipelago with 130-mph winds and heavy rains, USAF and ANG cargo aircraft fly more than 600 missions carrying 9,200 tons of relief supplies and 8,600 passengers.

13–29 September: As part of Operation Impressive Lift, AMC moves United Nations peacekeeping troops from Pakistan to Somalia. In 94 missions, USAF cargo aircraft move 974 passengers and 1,168 tons of equipment and supplies.

23–25 October: Two USAF C–130 Hercules transport aircraft evacuate 96 Americans from Liberia because of a civil war there.

25 October: A USAF C–141 Starlifter evacuates Americans and other foreign nationals from Tajikistan because of civil disturbances in the former Soviet republic.

4–11 November: Five USAF aircraft, four C–5 Galaxies, and one C–141 Starlifter transport 236 tons of flour from the United States to Armenia to relieve food shortages after the collapse of the Soviet Union and its centralized economy.

30 November: Two 62d Airlift Wing C–141s collide in midair and crash in Montana during a nighttime air refueling mission.

6–20 December: After a flood in Pakistan, six USAF C–5 Galaxy missions airlift 415 tons of engineering vehicles and equipment to Islamabad.

9 December–3 May 1993: Operation Restore Hope supports United Nations peacekeeping efforts in Somalia. AMC flies more than 1,000 airlift missions, carrying more than 50,000 passengers and 40,000 short tons of cargo. AFRES crews fly 190 sorties, carrying 1,076 passengers and more than 1,500 tons of cargo.

15 December: England AFB; Eaker AFB, Arkansas; and George AFB close.

16 December: On a night flight, a 668th Bomb Squadron B–52 loses two engines when one explodes and damages its neighbor. At about the same time, two more engines on the same side of the aircraft flame out. Frantically maneuvering with all four engines on the left side of the aircraft shut down, the crew is able to restart the two flamed-out engines and land safely. For this extraordinary feat, the crew will receive the Mackay Trophy.

27 December: A USAF F–16 Fighting Falcon shoots down an Iraqi MiG–25 while patrolling a United Nations no-fly zone near the Iraqi border.

1993

3 January: Presidents George Bush of the United States and Boris Yeltsin of Russia sign the second Strategic Arms Reduction Treaty (START II), the most far-reaching nuclear arms reduction pact in history. The agreement calls for the United States and Russia to eliminate all ICBMs carrying multiple, independently targetable reentry vehicles and reduce the number of nuclear weapons carried by their bombers.

13 January: AMC begins airlifting forces to southwest Asia in support of Southern Watch II to enforce a no-fly zone in southern Iraq near the borders of Saudi Arabia and Kuwait.

13 January: President Bush orders punitive air strikes against 32 Iraqi missile sites and air defense command centers after an Iraqi troop foray across the newly demarcated border with Kuwait and active Iraqi surface-to-air missile sites are discovered south of the 32 degrees north latitude.

13 January: USAF Maj Susan Helms, a member of the space shuttle *Endeavour* crew, becomes the first U.S. military woman in space.

17 January: A USAF F–16 Fighting Falcon shoots down an Iraqi MiG over northern Iraq.

18 January: In response to being fired on, Provide Comfort F–4G Phantom IIs attack surface-to-air missile sites in northern Iraq. F–16 Fighting Falcons bomb an Iraqi airfield after being shot at by antiaircraft artillery batteries.

18 January: The United States, the United Kingdom, France, Canada, Germany, and other nations airlifting relief supplies to Sarajevo, Bosnia, establish a joint air operations cell in Zagreb, Croatia.

2 February: The U.S. Air Force begins aeromedical evacuation flights to transport noncombatant victims of the Bosnian war from Zagreb to the United States for medical treatment.

13 February–9 March: In Operation Provide Refuge, U.S. Air Force cargo aircraft transport tons of food and other relief supplies from Hawaii to Kwajalein Atoll in the Marshall Islands to sustain 535 Chinese who had taken refuge there after their ship had broken down in the mid-Pacific.

19 February: The 64th Flying Training Wing launches the first student sortie in the new T–1A Jayhawk trainer aircraft.

28 February: The 435th Airlift Wing begins the first Provide Promise airdrop missions over parts of eastern Bosnia, a haven for refugees who had fled their villages in the face of advancing Serb forces.

13–14 March: After a gigantic blizzard called the storm of the century swept over a third of the United States from the Gulf of Mexico to New England, Air Force helicopters of the 301st Rescue Squadron rescue 93 flood victims in Florida.

31 March: The United Nations Security Council authorizes a NATO-enforced no-fly zone over Bosnia to discourage the use of warplanes in the Bosnian civil war. Operation Deny Flight will begin on 5 April.

31 March: Myrtle Beach AFB, South Carolina, closes, and flying operations cease at MacDill AFB.

April: USAF units in Alaska participate in the first joint exercise with the Russian air force, a search and rescue exercise in Siberia.

28 April: Secretary of Defense Les Aspin announces a new policy that women will be allowed to serve in combat roles, which permits women USAF pilots to fly combat aircraft.

17–29 May: Twenty-four C–5 Galaxy and C–141 Starlifter missions transport United Nations troops and equipment to Cambodia to oversee that country's first free elections since 1970.

1 June: In conjunction with the reduction of forces in Germany, USAFE closes Wueschheim and Lindsey Air Stations.

11 June: USAF AC–130 Spectre gunships participate in a United Nations raid on Somali warlord forces in retaliation for a 5 June attack on United Nations forces in Mogadishu.

17 June: Lt Col Patricia Fornes assumes command of the 740th Missile Squadron at Minot AFB. She is the first woman commander of a combat missile squadron.

29 June: The OC–135B Open Skies reconnaissance aircraft is successfully tested at Wright-Patterson AFB. It will be used under an international treaty that allows surveillance over other treaty nations.

30 June: Wurtsmith AFB closes after being an active military installation since 1924.

1 July: Air Training Command is redesignated the Air Education and Training Command (AETC), to which Air University, now ceasing to be a major command, is assigned. AETC activates the 392d Space and Missile Training Squadron at Vandenberg AFB, combining missile and space training that had been conducted by ACC and Air Training Command squadrons at separate bases.

1 July: The Twentieth Air Force, which is responsible for day-to-day operation of the nation's ICBM force, transfers from ACC to Air Force Space Command.

1 July: The ACC transfers Vandenberg AFB to AFSPACECOM, which activates the Fourteenth Air Force to perform missile warning, space surveillance, and launch and satellite control.

5–12 July: USAF cargo aircraft airlift American soldiers and their equipment from Germany to Macedonia to help United Nations forces prevent the spread of fighting in the former Yugoslavia.

11 July–1 August: One of the worst floods in American history inundates 16,000 square miles in eight Midwestern states along the upper Mississippi and lower Missouri Rivers. The Air Force responds by airlifting almost 800 tons of relief equipment and supplies, including water purification units and 1 million empty sandbags, on C–5 Galaxy and C–141 Starlifter aircraft.

19 July: DOD lifts a 50-year ban on homosexuals in the military by establishing a "don't ask, don't tell" policy, although it continues to forbid homosexual conduct in the military.

6 August: Dr. Sheila E. Widnall is sworn in as Secretary of the Air Force, becoming the first woman armed services secretary.

11–15 August: After a flood in Nepal washes out bridges, three 436th Airlift Wing C–5 Galaxies airlift at least 190 tons of bridge components from England.

20 August: USAFE turns over RAF Woodbridge to the British.

27 September: Gen James H. Doolittle, who led the first air raid on Tokyo and commanded the Eighth Air Force during World War II, dies at the age of 96.

30 September: The following U.S. Air Force bases close: Chanute AFB, Mather AFB, Williams AFB, Bergstrom AFB, and Carswell AFB. Additionally, USAFE turns over RAF Bentwaters to the British.

1 October: AFRES activates its first B–52 Stratofortress unit, the 93d Bomb Squadron, at Barksdale AFB.

2–4 October: After earthquakes hit central India, two AMC C–5 Galaxies airlift 1,000 rolls of plastic sheeting, 950 tents, 18,550 five-gallon water containers, 22 pallets of blankets, and other relief supplies to Bombay.

3–4 October: Despite enemy fire and his own injuries, USAF pararescueman TSgt Tim Wilkerson treats injured U.S. Army Rangers during a battle in Mogadishu, Somalia. For his heroism, he earns the Air Force Cross.

5–13 October: After a 15-hour pitched battle between U.S. Army Rangers and forces loyal to Mohammed Farah Aidid in Mogadishu, USAF C–5 Galaxy and C–141 Starlifter aircraft transport 1,300 troops, 18 M–1 Abrams tanks, and 44 Bradley infantry fighting vehicles from the United States to

Somalia in nine days. The operation is nicknamed Restore Hope II.

8 October: Operation Provide Promise, the airlift of humanitarian relief supplies to Bosnia, surpasses in duration (but not in tonnage or missions) the Berlin Airlift, becoming the longest sustained relief operation in USAF history.

October–November: When forest fires burn more than 167,000 acres in southern California, six AFRES and ANG C–130 Hercules aircraft help dispense over 1,000 tons of fire retardant.

November: Lt Col Betty Mullis becomes the first woman to command an AFRES flying unit, the 336th Air Refueling Squadron.

2–13 December: USAF Col Richard O. Covey pilots the space shuttle *Endeavour* on a mission that repairs the $2 billion Hubble Space Telescope.

8 December: The U.S. Air Force destroys the first of 450 LGM–30F Minuteman II missile silos scheduled for demolition under the 1991 Strategic Arms Reduction Treaty.

17 December: The first B–2 Spirit bomber arrives at Whiteman AFB, Missouri. The B–2 is the first "stealth" heavy bomber.

1994

January: Hungary, Romania, and Bulgaria grant overflight rights for F–16 Fighting Falcons deploying from Germany to Turkey, saving them two hours of flight time. This is the first flight of USAF fighters on an operational mission over these countries since World War II.

4 January: A C–130 Hercules aircraft squadron composed of AFRES and ANG personnel joins Operation Provide Promise to deliver relief supplies to Bosnia. It is called "Delta Squadron" and operates from Rhein-Main AB under the 435th Airlift Wing.

10 January: Crewmen from a 56th Rescue Squadron HH–60G Pave Hawk helicopter free six sailors from their damaged tugboat off the coast of Iceland, earning the Mackay Trophy.

13 January: The final F–15 Eagle of the 32d Fighter Group departs Soesterberg AB, ending 40 years of U.S. Air Force operations in the Netherlands.

17–25 January: After an earthquake strikes the Los Angeles area on 17 January, six AMC C–5 Galaxy and C–141 Starlifter missions transport 270 disaster specialists and 340,000 pounds of cargo, including fire trucks, generators, and communications vans, to southern California.

25 January: A USAF Titan II booster launches the unmanned space probe *Clementine I* toward the moon. This is the first American lunar mission since *Apollo 17* in 1972.

30 January: The U.S. Air Force inactivates the 717th AB Squadron and closes Ankara AS, Turkey.

February: USAF aircraft deploy to France for the first time in more than 20 years. The five KC–135 Stratotankers fly from French bases to refuel aircraft patrolling airspace over Bosnia-Herzegovina in Operation Deny Flight.

5 February: For the first time, an all-AFRES crew flies one of the new C–17 Globemaster IIIs. The crew comes from the 315th Airlift Wing's 317th Airlift Squadron.

5 February: After a mortar attack on Sarajevo's central market that killed 68 people and wounded 200 more, President Clinton sends a U.S. medical team and four C–130 Hercules aircraft to Sarajevo to evacuate the wounded to an Army hospital in Germany.

7 February: A Titan IV missile boosts the first Military Strategic and Tactical Relay satellite into geostationary orbit.

10 February: Lt Jeannie Flynn, the first woman selected for USAF combat pilot training, completes training in an F–15E Eagle.

18 February: The last F–4G Wild Weasels in Europe leave Spangdahlem AB for Nellis AFB.

25 February: In preparation for the closing of Bitburg AB in Germany, F–15 Eagle aircraft of the 53d Fighter Squadron move to Spangdahlem AB. The last F–15s will depart Bitburg in mid-March.

28 February: Two USAF F–16 Fighting Falcon aircraft of the 86th Fighter Wing shoot down four Serb Galeb attack aircraft over Bosnia during the first combat in NATO history. The F–16s operate as part of Operation Deny Flight over Bosnia-Herzegovina.

March: The U.S. Air Force begins training students in the T–3A flight screening aircraft that replaces the T–41 Mescalero. The Air Force has used the T–41 since 1964 to screen prospective pilots for undergraduate pilot training.

March: The U.S. Air Force begins flight testing F–16 Fighting Falcon launches of the AGM–84 Harpoon antiship missile at Edwards AFB.

13 March: The first Taurus booster launches two military satellites from Vandenberg AFB.

18 March: Norton AFB, California, closes after 52 years of operation.

25 March: The last American military personnel depart Mogadishu on a C–5 Galaxy, ending Operation Restore Hope and American military involvement in Somalia.

31 March: The first two F–16 Fighting Falcons from Ramstein AB arrive at Aviano AB. The next day, NATO names Aviano a main operating base. It will become a key airfield for operations over the former Yugoslavia.

April: The U.S. Air Force removes the last of 150 LGM–30F Minuteman II missiles from Ellsworth AFB, implementing part of the Strategic Arms Reduction Treaty between the United States and Russia.

6–12 April: In Operation Distant Runner, USAF airplanes transport Americans and other foreign citizens from Bujumbura, Burundi, to Nairobi, Kenya, when civil violence forces them to leave Rwanda.

10 April: Two USAF F–16 Fighting Falcons strike a Bosnian Serb command post near Gorazde in the former Yugoslavia after Bosnian Serbs attack United Nations personnel in the enclave. This is the first close air support mission of Operation Deny Flight and the first NATO air-to-ground bombing in history.

14 April: Two 53d Fighter Squadron F–15 Eagles mistakenly shoot down two U.S. Army UH–60 Black Hawk helicopters over northern Iraq, killing 26 people, including 15 Americans.

3 May: The last B–52G Stratofortress goes into storage at Davis-Monthan AFB. B–52Hs continue to serve in the Air Force.

6 May: 1st Lt Leslie DeAnn Crosby graduates from the ANG's F–16 Fighting Falcon training course in Tucson, Arizona, becoming the first AFRES woman fighter pilot.

7–9 May: After civil war erupts in Yemen, six USAF aircraft evacuate 623 people, including 448 Americans, from Yemen to Saudi Arabia.

8 May: Five C–141 Starlifters begin flying humanitarian airlift missions from Germany to Bosnia in support of Operation Provide Promise, supplementing the earlier C–130 Hercules flights. The C–141 Provide Promise flights will end on 26 July after delivering 7,000 tons of cargo to Sarajevo.

11–17 May: Air Force C–141 Starlifter cargo aircraft deliver 239 tons of relief supplies from Turkey to Tanzania for hundreds of thousands of Rwandan refugees who have fled tribal warfare in Rwanda. Part of a joint operation called Provide Assistance, this cargo includes 10,000 rolls of plastic sheeting and 100,000 blankets.

22–30 June: AMC C–5 Galaxies and C–141 Starlifters transport armored vehicles from Germany to Uganda for United Nations forces deploying to Rwanda.

26 June: A 60th Military Airlift Wing C–5 Galaxy airlifts a 34-ton magnetic resonance imaging system to Chernobyl, Ukraine, to help medical personnel treating victims of a 1986 nuclear accident.

30 June: USAFE ends its presence in Berlin, 46 years after the beginning of the Berlin airlift, with the inactivation of Detachment 1, 435th Airlift Wing.

June–September: Fires consume more than 2 million acres of forest and brush in six western states. Eight AFRES and ANG C–130 Hercules aircraft from the 302d Airlift Wing and the 145th and 153d Airlift Groups dispense nearly 5 million gallons of fire-retardant chemicals to fight the fires.

July: McDonnell Douglas delivers the final F–15 Eagle fighter to the U.S. Air Force.

July: The 507th Air Refueling Group airlifts 1,000 pounds of supplies from Oklahoma to Georgia to relieve the victims of flooding from Tropical Storm Alberto. Personnel from Robins and Moody Air Force Bases also participate in relief efforts.

1 July: The Kansas ANG's 184th Bomb Group becomes the first ANG unit equipped with the B–1B Lancer.

21 July: A USAF C–141 Starlifter flying Operation Provide Promise missions over Bosnia is hit by small arms fire near Sarajevo. Despite more than 25 holes in the fuselage and wings, the airplane returns safely to Rhein-Main AB. All flights to Sarajevo are temporarily suspended.

21 July: USAFE fighter operations at Ramstein AB end when the last 86th Fighter Wing F–16 Fighting Falcon departs for Aviano AB.

24 July–6 October: USAF aircraft participate in Operation Support Hope, flying humanitarian relief supplies to Rwandan refugees in Zaire.

2 August: Two 2d Bomb Wing B–52 Stratofortresses set a world record circumnavigating the earth during a global-power mission to Kuwait. The 47-hour flight takes five aerial refuelings.

3 August: USAF launches a research satellite from a B–52 Stratofortress, using a Pegasus rocket.

4 August: Brig Gen Susan L. Pamerleau becomes the first woman commander of the Air Force Reserve Officer Training Corps.

5 August: Two USAF A–10 Thunderbolt II jets destroy an armored vehicle near Sarajevo after Serbs seize heavy weapons from a United Nations compound. The weapons are later returned.

24–25 August: As a typhoon approaches Johnston Island in the Pacific, USAF airplanes help evacuate more than 1,000 people.

25–31 August: The United States and Ukraine hold a joint Open Skies trial flight. The Open Skies agreement, which both nations signed, allows them to conduct reconnaissance flights over each other's territory.

31 August–8 September: Russian, American, British, and French military forces withdraw from Berlin after 49 years in the continuing effort to end the Cold War.

31 August–10 September: In an operation called Safe Haven, the Air Force and other military services transport Cuban and Haitian refugees from overcrowded camps at the American base at Guantanamo Bay, Cuba, to Panama for temporary shelter.

September: A B–52 Stratofortress, a B–1B Lancer, and a KC–10 Extender land at Poltava AB, the Ukraine. This is the first time since World War II that American bombers land in Ukraine. B–17 Flying Fortresses flew there 50 years earlier on shuttle bombing missions against Nazi targets in eastern Europe.

19 September: In a noncombat operation called Uphold Democracy, U.S. military forces go to Haiti to restore the country's democratically elected president and stem the flow of Haitian refugees to the United States. The Air Force provides airlift for the peaceful invasion.

29–30 September: USAFE vacates Soesterberg AB, the Netherlands, and RAF Upper Heyford, United Kingdom, marking further reduction of American air bases in Europe after the Cold War.

30 September: The following Air Force bases close: Grissom AFB; Loring AFB; Lowry AFB; Richards-Gebaur AFB, Missouri; and Rickenbacker ANG Base, Ohio.

4 October: F–16 Fighting Falcons replace the last F–4 Wild Weasel aircraft performing the suppression of enemy air defense missions.

6 October: Operation Support Hope, which includes airlift of relief supplies to Rwandan refugees in central Africa, is terminated.

10 October: After Iraqi troops mass near the Kuwaiti border, Air Force cargo planes begin flying more U.S. forces to the Persian Gulf region in an operation called Vigilant Warrior. During October, the USAF increases its presence in the Persian Gulf from 77 to 270 aircraft, including F–15E Eagle, F–16 Fighting Falcon, and A–10 Thunderbolt II aircraft.

14–16 October: Two C–17 Globemaster IIIs transport military equipment and supplies from Langley AFB to Saudi Arabia in the Persian Gulf region in the aircraft's first operational mission.

30 October: A C–141 Starlifter airlifts 20 tons of medical supplies, blankets, and tarpaulins, from Kadena AB to Vladivostok, Russia, to relieve the victims of a Siberian flood.

31 October–1 November: Two B–1B Lancer bombers fly nonstop from Ellsworth AFB to a bombing range in Kuwait and back. The 25-hour mission marks the first time B–1s fly to the Persian Gulf.

6–8 November: Two USAF C–141 Starlifters transport 37 tons of plastic sheeting, blankets, and communications equipment to Egypt after flash floods inundate as many as 70 villages.

21–23 November: USAF and NATO aircraft bomb Serb targets, including an airfield and missile sites, in the former Yugoslavia. NATO launches the raids in retaliation for a Serb attack on Bihac. This is the largest NATO operation to date.

21–23 November: As part of Project Sapphire, C–5s transport more than 1,300 pounds of highly enriched uranium from the former Soviet Republic of Kazakhstan to the United States to protect it from terrorists, smugglers, and unfriendly governments.

17–21 December: A 94th Airlift Wing C–130 Hercules crew delivers five pallets of clothing, furniture, books, beds, and plastic windows, plus a refrigerator to Albania for orphan shelters.

29 December: Two helicopter crews from the 56th Rescue Squadron help rescue eight Dutch mariners from a sinking ship off the coast of Iceland.

1995

17 January: AMC declares the 17th Airlift Squadron the first operational C–17 Globemaster III squadron. Simultaneously, Gen Robert L. Rutherford, commander of AMC, approves use of the new C–17 Globemaster III for routine missions.

19 January: C–130 Hercules transport planes from the 374th Airlift Wing at Yokota AB begin flying humanitarian airlift missions to help the victims of an earthquake that struck southwestern Japan on 17 January.

1–20 February: After riots at Cuban refugee camps in Panama, USAF C–5 Galaxy, C–141 Starlifter, and C–130 Hercules aircraft transport about 7,300 Cubans to Guantanamo Bay Naval AS, Cuba, in Operation Safe Passage.

3 February: USAF Lt Col Eileen M. Collins becomes the first woman space shuttle pilot.

3–10 February: Eight C–141 Starlifters transport 410 Nepalese troops from Katmandu to Haiti for service with United Nations peacekeeping forces.

5 March: As part of the Strategic Arms Reduction Treaty, Russian weapons inspectors arrive at Malmstrom AFB to monitor LGM–30F Minuteman II dismantlement.

10 March: The 11th Space Warning Squadron becomes the first squadron able to warn battlefield commanders of incoming theater ballistic missiles, such as Scuds fired by Iraq during the Persian Gulf War.

16 March: A HH–60 Pave Hawk helicopter crew from the 56th Rescue Squadron stationed at Keflavik, Iceland, saves three Icelanders caught in a blizzard while skiing.

24 March: The last USAF Atlas E booster, a converted ICBM from the 1960s, launches a satellite into polar orbit from Vandenberg AFB.

31 March: 2d Lt Kelly Flinn begins training to become the first woman bomber pilot in the U.S. Air Force. Following graduation, she will fly B–52s at Minot AFB.

8 April: After an Air Force C–130 Hercules aircraft delivers flour to Sarajevo, Bosnia, as part of Operation Provide Promise, it is hit 12 times by small arms fire during takeoff return to Italy. The airplane completes the flight safely.

19 April: A powerful car bomb explodes at a federal building in Oklahoma City, killing 169 people, including 19 children, and injuring more than 400 others. The Air Force responds with an airlift of firefighters, urban search and rescue teams, investigators, and medical personnel from all over the United States to Oklahoma. Nearby Tinker AFB also provides rescuers with vehicles, blood, rain gear, boots, hard hats, flashlights, batteries, and bomb-sniffing dogs.

27 April: Air Force Space Command declares the GPS satellite constellation fully operational. The system provides accurate geographical coordinates.

8–11 May: ANG units rescue thousands of flood victims after more than 22 inches of rain fall over parts of Louisiana in less than two days.

10–17 May: After an outbreak of the deadly Ebola virus in central Africa, a 349th Air Mobility Wing C–141 Starlifter crew delivers more than a ton of medical supplies to Zaire. During the same month, a 60th Airlift Wing C–5 Galaxy takes a ton of medical supplies to Kinshasa, Zaire.

25–26 May: USAF aircraft participate in NATO attacks on Serb military bunkers in Bosnia to halt Serb artillery attacks against Sarajevo.

1 June: The United States and Portugal sign a treaty allowing the United States to use Lajes Field in the Azores for another five years. Lajes has become a major staging base for USAF aircraft deploying to the Middle East.

2–3 June: Two USAF B–1B Lancer bombers fly around the world in a record 36 hours, 13 minutes, 36 seconds, refueling in flight six times. For flying the longest nonaugmented crew sortie to date, the crew will receive the 1996 Mackay Trophy.

2–8 June: After a surface-to-air missile downs his F–16 Fighting Falcon fighter over Bosnia, USAF Capt Scott O'Grady evades capture by hostile forces for six days until he is rescued by U.S. Marine Corps helicopters.

27 June: Lockheed Martin begins assembling the first production model of the F–22—a stealthy, advanced tactical fighter that will eventually replace the F–15 Eagle.

30 June–10 August: USAF C–5 Galaxies and C–141 Starlifters airlift British and Dutch forces to Croatia to support the United Nations in an operation called Quick Lift.

23 July: A 433d Airlift Wing C–5 Galaxy crew airlifts 28 pallets of medical supplies, blankets, clothes, furniture, and a military ambulance to relieve economic suffering in Byelorussia.

31 July: The last remaining LGM–30F Minuteman II missile wing, the 351st Missile Wing, is inactivated at Whiteman AFB.

13 August: A 60th Air Mobility Wing C–5 Galaxy transports 75 tons of food from Germany to Croatia to feed victims of the war in the former Yugoslavia.

17 August: The E–8C joint surveillance target attack radar system (JSTARS) aircraft begins flight tests. The sophisticated radar plane will replace experimental JSTARS aircraft used during the Persian Gulf War.

20–21 August: A C–5 Galaxy flies 75 tons of food from Ramstein AB to Zagreb, Croatia, for refugees of the civil war in the former Yugoslavia.

25–29 August: C–17 Globemaster III cargo aircraft participate in their first major exercise. Eleven C–17s from the 315th and 437th Airlift Wings move almost 300 tons of troops and equipment to Kuwait.

30 August: NATO aircraft, including USAF airplanes, begin air strikes on Serb positions in Bosnia in support of the United Nations. The operation is called Deliberate Force.

1 September: The SR–71 Blackbird, fastest aircraft in the world, returns to active service. It was removed from the

USAF inventory in 1990 when planners assumed that satellites could perform the strategic reconnaissance mission.

14–30 September: USAF airlifts more than 30 tons of medical supplies from Charleston AFB to Hanoi, Vietnam. This is the first American humanitarian airlift to Vietnam since the war there ended in 1975.

15–21 September: After Hurricane Marilyn devastated the eastern Caribbean Sea, USAF, AFRES, and ANG cargo aircraft airlift 996 tons of relief cargo and 85 passengers to the Virgin Islands. This is the first disaster relief operation employing C–17 Globemaster III aircraft.

22 September: After 53 years of operation, Griffiss AFB closes.

30 September: The 93d Bombardment Wing, first B–52 wing in the SAC, inactivates after more than 47 years of continuous service. At the same time, its home base at Castle AFB closes. Also closing after more than 41 years, is Plattsburgh AFB, New York, a former SAC base.

October: The first C–130J, an advanced-technology version of the venerable Hercules transport, rolls out of its assembly plant at Marietta, Georgia.

1 October: CMSgt Carol Smits becomes the first female senior enlisted advisor of the AFRES.

4 October: Hurricane Opal damages Eglin AFB and Hurlburt Field in Florida with winds over 110 mph. Most of the aircraft escape damage by evacuating to other bases.

16–17 October: The 53d Weather Reconnaissance Squadron, which had been monitoring the strength and movement of Hurricane Roxanne in the Gulf of Mexico, searches for survivors of a Mexican pipe-laying barge sunk by the hurricane. One crew finds a survivor in a raft and radios his position to the Coast Guard, which subsequently rescues 23 more of the 236 survivors.

28 October–18 December: In an operation called Vigilant Sentinel, the Air Force first tests the air expeditionary force concept. F–16 Fighting Falcons of the 20th Fighter Wing and the 347th Wing deploy to Bahrain.

1 November: Wright-Patterson AFB hosts the presidents of Bosnia, Croatia, and Serbia for peace talks designed to end the war in the former Yugoslavia.

6 December: USAF transports begin airlifting American troops and equipment into Bosnia in support of a NATO peacekeeping operation called Joint Endeavor. The operation seeks to implement a peace agreement initialed by the presidents of Bosnia, Croatia, and Serbia at Wright-Patterson AFB and signed later in December in Paris.

1996

4 January: Operation Provide Promise, the longest sustained humanitarian airlift in history, officially ends, after delivering 160,536 metric tons of relief cargo since July 1992. The U.S. Air Force flew 4,597 of the 12,895 sorties. On 9 January there will be a commemorative final flight.

26 January: CMSgt Patricia M. Hoffman, the Air Force's most senior-ranking enlisted woman, retires at Randolph AFB with more than 30 years of service.

14 February: The joint surveillance and target attack radar system E–8A flies its 50th mission in support of Operation Joint Endeavor, a peacekeeping operation in the former Yugoslavia. This surpasses the JSTARS record of 49 missions during Operation Desert Storm.

Late March: The last F–4 Phantom aircraft in the active duty Air Force goes into storage at Davis-Monthan AFB. The F–4 has served the Air Force for more than 30 years.

29 March: The Tier III Minus Dark Star, a stealthy drone designed for high-altitude, long-duration reconnaissance missions over hostile territory, completes its first test flight at Edwards AFB.

29 March: Vice President Albert Gore announces that the United States will open the GPS, a constellation of Air Force satellites, to full commercial access.

3 April: A 76th Airlift Squadron CT–43 transport airplane crashes into a hillside near Dubrovnik, Croatia. Among the

35 killed is Commerce Secretary Ronald Brown, who was on an economic development mission to the former Yugoslavia.

9–25 April: USAF units participate in Operation Assured Response, which evacuates more than 2,000 noncombatants from Liberia during civil unrest there. Air Force aircraft, including MH–53 Pave Low helicopters, KC–135 Stratotankers, C–130 Hercules cargo airplanes, MC–130 Combat Talons, and AC–130 Spectre aircraft, fly 94 missions.

15 April: Interservice undergraduate navigator training becomes fully joint as Air Force student navigators and student naval flight officers are combined at Randolph AFB into a single class with a single syllabus. During the same month, Air Force and Navy electronic warfare officer training are combined at Pensacola Naval AS and the Naval Technical Training Center at Corry Field, Florida.

17 April: Operation Uphold Democracy, which began in September 1994 in Haiti, ends. Only one American soldier was killed by hostile fire during the 18-month operation in which U.S. military forces oversaw the dismantling of a military dictatorship.

18 April: For the first time, C–17 Globemaster III aircraft airlift huge MH–53J Pave Low special operations helicopters. Two C–17s carry two of the helicopters from Sierra Leone in Africa to England, saving time and refuelings.

30 April: USAF reveals the Tacit Blue test airplane that was used secretly to test stealth technology until 1985. With a 56-foot wingspan, Tacit Blue aircraft furnished the technology used to produce the B–2 Spirit bomber.

1 May: A German officer assumes command of a German tactical training center at Holloman AFB. This is the first time a foreigner has commanded a unit at an Air Force base within the United States.

31 May: The U.S. Air Force awards contracts to produce 80 more C–17 Globemaster III transport aircraft over the course of seven years. Worth $16.2 billion, these military contracts are the largest ever awarded. The 80 planes will complete a fleet of 120 C–17s, which are replacing the Air Force's aging fleet of C–141 Starlifters.

6 June: Lt Col Kai Lee Norwood, the first woman commander of a group that maintains Air Force missiles, assumes command of the 91st Logistics Group.

21 June: Cmdr David Cheslak becomes the first Navy flight officer to command an Air Force squadron when he assumes command of the 562d Flying Training Squadron at Randolph AFB where Air Force and Navy personnel are experiencing joint navigation training.

25 June: Terrorists bomb the Khobar Towers near King Abdul-Aziz AB in Saudi Arabia, killing 19 Air Force personnel and injuring some 300 other Americans. It is the worst terrorist attack against American military personnel since the 1983 bombing of a U.S. Marine barracks in Beirut, Lebanon. The Americans are in Saudi Arabia as part of Operation Southern Watch to deter Iraqi aggression against Kuwait and Saudi Arabia.

1 July: For the first time, an Air Force crew flies an EA–6B Prowler off the deck of an aircraft carrier, the USS *Constellation*, in the Pacific Ocean. The Navy's EA–6B will replace the EF–111 as an Air Force radar-jamming aircraft.

19 July–4 August: During the Centennial Olympic Games in Atlanta, USAF personnel help provide security.

27 July: The Air Force hosts an F–111 retirement celebration at a plant in Fort Worth, Texas, where the first Aardvark rolled out over 30 years earlier. At about the same time, the last F–111 unit in the Air Force, the 524th Fighter Squadron at Cannon AFB, New Mexico, converts to F–16 Fighting Falcons.

Late August: Four C–130s, two each from the 146th and 302d Airlift Wings, fight severe forest fires in northern California.

2–3 September: As part of Operation Desert Strike, the U.S. Air Force flies B-52 Stratofortresses to the Middle East and launches 13 cruise missiles against military targets in Iraq. This is in response to an Iraqi troop seizure of the city of Irbil, located in an American-protected zone for Kurds.

3 September: The 11th Reconnaissance Squadron becomes the first Air Force unit to operate the Predator, an unmanned aerial vehicle designed for aerial surveillance and reconnaissance. Flights over Bosnia-Herzegovina help the United States to ensure a peace agreement there.

4 September: A C–141 Starlifter of the 305th Air Mobility Wing, McGuire AFB, evacuates 30 passengers from Bujumbura, Burundi, to Nairobi, Kenya, to remove them from the danger of a civil war in Burundi.

5 September: To relieve the victims of Hurricane Fran, C–130 Hercules aircraft and crews from the 145th Airlift Wing begin airlifting engineers, security police, generators, mobile kitchens, and showers to the Raleigh and Wilmington areas of North Carolina.

14 September: Air Force Special Operations forces help provide security for the first elections in Bosnia since the end of a civil war that erupted shortly after the republic declared independence from Yugoslavia.

16–19 September: After hostile forces in northern Iraq drove Kurds out of their villages, USAF chartered flights to airlift 2,134 refugees from the Middle East to Andersen AFB.

30 September: The Seventeenth Air Force inactivates after more than 43 years of service with USAFE. Two other numbered Air Forces remain in Europe.

21 November: Secretary of the Air Force Dr. Sheila Widnall and Chief of Staff of the Air Force Gen Ronald R. Fogleman publicly release the *Global Reach—Global Power* engagement strategic planning framework—a position paper for Air Force power projection in the twenty-first century.

1997

9 April: Rollout of the Lockheed-Martin-Boeing F–22 Raptor stealth air superiority fighter designed to secure air dominance for the United States in the twenty-first century.

Rollout of F–22 Raptor stealth air superiority fighter at Marietta, Georgia, 9 April 1997, marks a new departure in the quest for air supremacy—the drive for air dominance.

ISBN 0-16-049145-2